AN EPIC TUDOR
JOURNEY

An Epic Tudor Journey

*John Leland's Itinerary
of Northern Wales*

Derek Williams

© Text: Derek Williams
First published in 2008

ISBN: 978-1-84524-121-6

Cover design: Sian Parri

Published by
Llygad Gwalch, Ysgubor Plas, Llwyndyrys,
Pwllheli, Gwynedd LL53 6NG
℡ 01758 750432   🖷 01758 750438
✆ gai@llygadgwalch.com
Web site: www.carreg-gwalch.co.uk

For my wife
Cerys Ann

CONTENTS

PREFACE

John Leland was given a royal commission in 1533 to search the libraries – monastic and cathedral – in England and Wales for manuscripts of historical interest. Fortunately he was interested also in the contemporary geography – towns, villages, farming, woodland, castles and especially rivers and coastal features. There is evidence that he travelled in Wales during the summers of 1536-39 and though the chronology of his travels is uncertain he seems to have been there before some of the major monasteries were 'dissolved' and their doors closed (1536-7). He says in his 'Itinerary' that he was given local information by the Abbot of Whitland and a monk at Strata Florida. He was notably reticent about monasteries such as Valle Crucis (Llangollen) and Maenan (near Llanrwst) usually mentioning only their position and the farming around them. He clearly did not wish to give offence to Thomas Cromwell, Henry VIII's chief minister who was responsible for their destruction and confiscation of land, property and goods. Leland was travelling at a time when Henry had broken from the Roman Catholic Church but the parish churches continued using the Latin liturgy and pilgrimages and veneration of saints were still a feature of religious life. In the churches the medieval wall-paintings gave a splash of colour to the interior and had not yet been covered over as part of the Protestant Reformation.

Leland kept notes recording his journey from the English border to the Llŷn peninsula; these notes and a copy made later by John Stow have survived and are now in the Bodleian Library, Oxford. These notes were transcribed by Lucy T. Smith in five volumes in 1906-10 and she compiled a section on his 'Itinerary in Wales'. She had a Welsh scholar to advise her on Welsh place names which were often incorrectly spelled by Leland.

When Leland set off from Maelor Saesneg he must have had information and a list of houses and their owners where he could get help and hospitality as an important Royal official. He was travelling on horseback at about ten miles a day and not having a map needed local guides. Unfortunately his notes do not include personal details so we have to rely on the geographical order of the place-names as well as a few directional clues such as *'this way'* and *'left-hand side'*. He does name specific houses and their owners and knew exactly those which belonged to families who had fought and supported Henry VII at the Battle of Bosworth and helped to establish the Tudor Dynasty. He sometimes refers

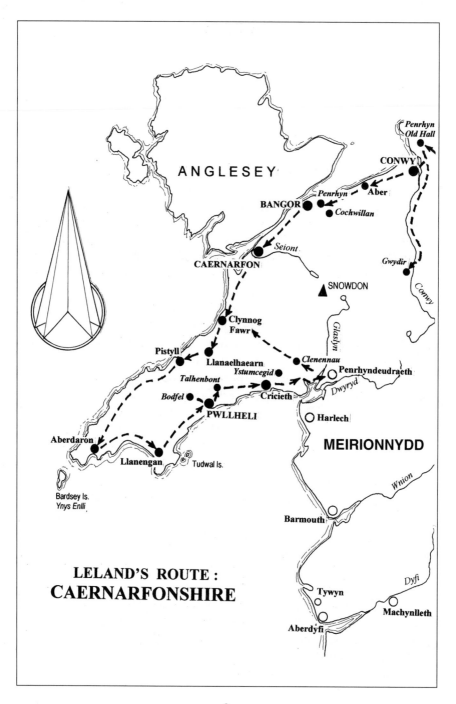

ANGLESEY

Penrhyn
Old Hall

CONWY

Penrhyn   Aber
BANGOR
Cochwillan

Gwydir

Seiont

CAERNARFON

Conwy

▲ SNOWDON

Clynnog
Fawr

Glaslyn

Pistyll

Clenennau

Llanaelhaearn

Ystumcegid   Penrhyndeudraeth

Talhenbont

Dwyryd

Bodfel   Cricieth

PWLLHELI

Harlech

MEIRIONNYDD

Aberdaron

Llanengan   Tudwal Is.

Wnion

Bardsey Is.
Ynys Enlli

Barmouth

LELAND'S ROUTE :
CAERNARFONSHIRE

Dyfi

Tywyn

Machynlleth

Aberdyfi

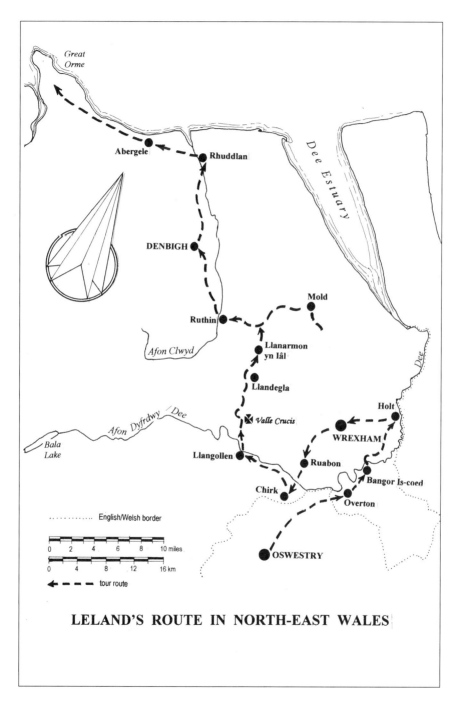

LELAND'S ROUTE IN NORTH-EAST WALES

by name to some people who gave him information such as *'Mr Rowland Griffith, of Anglesey, told me . . . '* He also shows appreciation of some of these houses such as:

ALTHREY HALL	*'a fair house'*
PENRHYN OLD HALL	*'an ancient stone house'*
GWYDIR	*'a pretty place'*

In the course of following Leland's journey it is reassuring to see the survival of many houses and churches such as the finely-restored half-timbered house at Althrey near Bangor-on-Dee. The Broncoed Tower at Mold is one of the finest late-Medieval houses in northern Wales and would be instantly recognised by Leland and is still in the hands of descendants of the 1536-7 owners – John Wynn ap Robert. The moat at New Hall, Chirk, with its revetted stone masonry, its bridge over the moat and its spring-fed water is in perfect condition. Even ruins in Leland's day have survived! Ewloe Castle: *'a ruinous castle or pile called Castell Yollo'* thanks to the custodianship of CADW is one of the finest ruins in northern Wales. At Ruabon Church which Leland must have visited to see the fine alabaster effigy of John ap Elis Eyton and his wife he also saw the medieval wall-painting which had not then been whitewashed over and 'lost' until 1870.

To fully understand Leland's text it is necessary to examine details in the field and use any local knowledge. One mystery was his reference to *'Llin Alen'* (Llyn Alun) as the source of the River Alun. The name does not appear on O.S. maps. The pool still exists and is known by the local farmers as the source of the Alun. A few miles downstream near Llandegla church Leland would have passed Tegla's Well then at the 'height' of its power to cure epilepsy. The well still retains its square-walled chamber with calcium-rich spring water still flowing strongly into the Alun. The local council have put up a signpost, and made a footpath and footbridge to the site of the well.

Further afield – in Llŷn – the churches such as Clynnog-fawr and Llanengan were given special attention by Leland and may have provided him with accommodation. They had both been almost completely rebuilt only a few years before his visit. At Clynnog he refers to *"the church, with cross-aisles, is almost as big as St David's but it is of a new work."*

Both had new towers and entrance porches and at Clynnog the porch with outer windows, a wooden floor and steps already provided living space for four canons. At Llanengan the porch over the entrance had windows and even a garderobe and was used to accommodate the custodian. Leland refers to a recent pilgrimage and its unique view of Bardsey Island must have impressed him.

By using the text and detailed field work it is possible to recreate the route taken by Leland in 1536-9.

ALTHREY HALL, Bangor on Dee
Over $^3/_4$ of its oak timbers had to be restored (by Tom Smith) over nine years

THE LONG MARCH TO BOSWORTH FIELD

Henry VII becomes King (1485)

By 1483 the dynastic struggle between the Lancastrians (red rose) and Yorkists (white) – the descendants of Edward III – known as the 'Wars of the Roses' reached a deadly climax. The King, Edward IV, died and his son and heir, Edward, was only twelve years old when a ruthless royal kinsman, Richard of Gloucester, seized the throne. He imprisoned Edward and his brother who were probably murdered ('the Princes in the Tower') and Richard III became King. This stirred Henry, Earl of Richmond, to claim the throne through his mother, Margaret Beaufort, who was married to Edmund Tudor. Henry and his brother, Jasper, had been exiled in France for many years and now collected a mercenary army of about 2000 men who set sail from Harfleur in Normandy. They arrived a little before sunset on August 7th at Mill Bay at the entrance to Milford Haven in Pembrokeshire. A great supporter was Rhys ap Thomas who had an army of retainers and owned eight castles including Carew Castle on a creek in the Haven. Henry also expected support from Wales because of his descent from the Tudor family from Anglesey. Rhys and Henry devised a plan to stage a forced march – sending scouts ahead – through Wales as they proceeded towards the English border. Rhys followed a route north-eastwards through Brecon, Llanidloes, Newtown, with the intention of meeting up with Henry's army at Long Mountain, three miles east of Welshpool. Henry's army mainly followed the coast through Haverfordwest on roads which were little better than tracks. By 9th August he completed the journey to Cardigan and is supposed to have had rest and refreshments at 'The

KING HENRY VII
Painted in 1505

The first gold sovereign of 1489 struck during the reign of Henry VII

Three Mariners' in the town. The journey led northwards where Henry is supposed to have stayed at a large house at Llwyn Dafydd and given a good welcome by Dafydd ap Ieuan to whom, later, he gave the 'Hirlas Horn' which was a drinking horn with a silver tip and stand with the royal crest. Stories such as this abound and on the following night (August 10th) he spent the night at Wern Newydd in the parish of Llanarth; a tablet in the bedroom claims to verify this event. The army was travelling at up to twenty miles a day and passing Aberystwyth they made their way up the Dyfi valley to Machynlleth and pitched camp five miles to the east at Mathafan. He was welcomed at the large farmhouse by the poet Dafydd Llwyd who later became an esquire (a status just below a knight) to Henry when he became King. The next stage took the army through the desolate Pass of Bwlchyfed to Castle Caereinion. Here Henry is supposed to have stayed at the old manor-house of Dolarddyn, half a mile north of the village. The main stage of the march neared its end in Wales on 13th August at Long Mountain three miles east of Welshpool. Here he met up with Rhys ap Thomas and received valuable reinforcements from northern Wales. One of these leaders was Rhys ap Maredudd from the Hiraethog area who led a group of soldiers and after Sir William Brandon was cut down at Bosworth Field he became the standard bearer to Henry. Another contingent was led by William ap Gruffydd of Cwchwillan near Bangor in the heart of 'Tudor country'. In the Bromfield area near Wrexham John ap Elis Eyton of Ruabon also took a prominent part in the battle.

From the rendezvous at Long Mountain the combined forces trekked eastwards to a fording point on the River Severn at Mountford and on 14th August the magistrates opened the gates to Shrewsbury. The army continued eastwards through Stafford where they had an interview with Sir William Stanley who was Henry's brother-in-law and had large estates with armed retainers in the North-West. They then entered Lichfield and were given a warm welcome and then at Atherstone he met Lord Stafford and Sir William Stanley who gave Henry their decisive support. On 21st

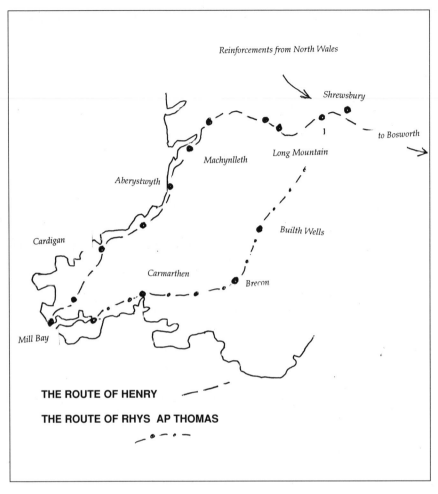

Routes of Henry Tudor a Rhys ap Thomas through Wales to the Battle of Bosworth in 1485

August the army encamped outside Market Bosworth and met Richard's army at Bosworth Field on the fateful 22nd August 1485. Richard was killed in the battle and Sir William Stanley placed the crown on the head of the new King – Henry VII. His close ally, Rhys ap Thomas, was made a Knight of the Garter on the battlefield.

After Bosworth Henry, having no standing army or police force, was anxious to reward the men who had supported him. His patronage took the form of grants of land, annuities and pensions. He also gave out offices such as Constables of Castles, Serjeant at Arms and bodyguards in the Royal Household. He reigned until 1509 and was succeeded by Henry VIII who was barely eighteen years of age. Henry VII had established the Tudor dynasty and was buried in the magnificent chapel which he built at Westminster Abbey with the emblem of the Beaufort portcullis and the double rose of the Tudors over his tomb.

When Leland set out on his visit to northern Wales in 1536-9 on the commission of Henry VIII he had full knowledge of the crucial episode leading up to Bosworth. He described his visit to Pembroke Castle which is *'very large and strong with double wards. In the outer ward I saw the chamber where King Henry the VII was born, in recognition of which a chimney has been recently built with the arms and badges of King Henry the VII'*.

Although he had serious misgivings and fears for his safety in some parts of northern Wales, as well as the practical problems of day-to-day travel, it was possible to choose a route through 'safe' territory where he could get lodging and hospitality as a Royal official. He must have had a list of the families with substantial houses who would offer him a good welcome. Bosworth Field was then a distant 50-year old memory but the sons of those who had fought there were anxious to show their continued support of the Tudor monarchy under Henry VIII.

'A RISK WORTH TAKING'

Rhys Ap Maredudd

As the events were unfolding at Milford Haven with Henry's landing in August 1485 Rhys ap Maredudd in the remote uplands of Hiraethog was making a decision to join Henry in his march across Wales to claim the throne of England. As his name 'Rhys Fawr' (Rhys the Great) implies he was of large build and was descended from the tribal lords of Hiraethog. He lived in the township of Tir Ifan which was part of the territory of the Knights' Hospitallers who had settled since the early 13th century at nearby Ysbyty Ifan. His house at Plas Iolyn was a substantial stone, three-storeyed tower with an adjoining hall (now a barn). Lying on a rock ridge it had a strategic site overlooking Merddwr valley just above its confluence with Afon Conwy. A remnant of the old tower survives with its basement cut into the rock and the ground floor having a recess and place for a fire. The entrance is through a narrow arched doorway and the nearby well was used until recently.

As a substantial landowner in the area Rhys had a band of armed retainers known as *'Gwŷr y wlad uchaf'* (men of the upland country) and he was prepared to deploy them in support of Henry Tudor. They marched southwards through Cerrigydrudion, Corwen and then, probably, through a low gap in the Berwyn Range to join Henry's army at Long Mountain near Welshpool. The army then marched eastwards to encounter Richard III at Bosworth. Here, due to the death in action of Sir William Brandon, Rhys took over as Standard Bearer for Henry and, according to tradition, killed Richard in the battle.

After the battle Rhys returned to Plas Iolyn and Henry's gratitude for his support led to a consolidation of his estates and wealth. His son, Robert, was educated at Oxford and became chaplain and cross-bearer to Cardinal Wolsey in the succeeding reign of Henry VIII. Robert was able to build a new house at Plas Iolyn which was extolled by the bards as a fine mansion alongside the now redundant tower. Robert ap Rhys's children adopted the surname 'Prys' or 'Price' at a time when the process of replacing *'ap'* (son of) by a settled surname spread even into the remote parts of Wales. This was accelerated by the requirement to keep parish records and the law courts after the Act of Union (1536). Priests and court officials found it easier to use the English-style surnames because they

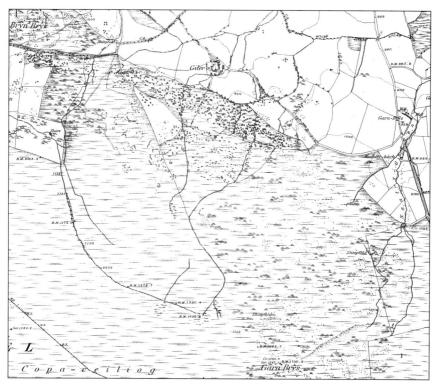

O.S. Map. 1879 Tre Brys Township
Bryn Brys – 105q Feet   Garn Brys – 1747 Feet
Bwlch Brys   Garn Brys – Farm

had little or no knowledge of the ancient Welsh traditions of genealogy. *'Ap Rhys'* became 'Prys' or 'Price' and Ellis Price, son of Robert, adopted the 'new' surname. He was educated at Cambridge and on his father's death (1534) succeeded to Plas Iolyn. He became a commissioner for northern Wales in the investigation of the monasteries prior to their 'dissolution' (1536). Locally he benefited from the disposal of monastic land and church benefices. He continued in Royal favour under Queen Elizabeth with land at Ysbyty Ifan (1560) granted to him and he extracted tithes for a wide area around Pentrefoelas and needed another barn (with a dated beam 1572). A poem written in 1572 states that Elis Prys had renewed the house at Plas Iolyn and went on to praise the finely-built walls, large wine cellars, glass windows, the dog-leg staircase and the hall that was as large as that of a palace.

Ysbyty Ifan Church

This is a very impressive brass plate for the memory of Robert Gethin grandson of Rhys ap Maredudd. It details his marriage to Anne, daughter of the Lord of Rhufoniog and their death in 1598. Their remains lie beneath the tablet in the remote church of Ysbyty Ifan. The upper plate was added by Robert's son Maurice Gethin and shows the white lion and red shield of the Lords of Hiraethog.

Alabaster Effigies in Ysbyty Ifan Church
Robert (son) – in foreground, Rhys ap Maredudd – middle,
Lowri, his wife – under window

Meanwhile the other grandsons of Rhys ap Maredudd – Cadwaladr and Robert Wyn Gethin – were granted land to build houses at Foelas and Cerniogiau respectively by Henry VIII. On 16th March 1545 they paid a nominal annual rent of £1.16s. 8d. for the land. Another house was built near Plas Iolyn at Gilar and, later, in the Dee valley at Rhiwlas near Bala.

By the end of the 16th century the Price family owned practically the whole valley of the upper Conwy from Ysbyty Ifan to Cerrigydrudion. Their wealth and authority is shown by the place names which are still shown on the O.S. maps:

GARN PRYS	–	the highest local summit
BRYN PRYS	–	a prominent hill
BWLCH PRYS		a pass

and numerous farm-names such as HENDRE PRYS and AELWYD PRYS.

It is certain that Leland knew of Rhys ap Maredudd's role at Bosworth and the continued support of Robert ap Rhys and Ellis Price to the Tudor monarchy. However he did not visit the area – it is possible that family matters were complicated after Robert's death in 1534. It was also an area which was then remote and cut off with no road links with the Conwy valley around Llanrwst and Gwydir Castle. Leland's brief comment on the area was *'Llanfair. . . this parish is called in Welsh Cerrigydrudion. It is very barren with oats grown only with much labour. There is abundant peat but no woodland. It is full of hills and bogs'*.

In Ysbyty Ifan church three alabaster effigies are those of Rhys ap Maredudd, his wife Lowri, and their eldest son, Robert, and were probably commissioned by, and placed there, by Dr Ellis Price.

'MY LABORIOUS JOURNEY AND COSTLY ENTERPRISE'

John Leland's Itinerary

John Leland was born c.1503 and related to Sir William Leyland of Morleys Hall, Leigh in Lancashire. After the death of his parents he was adopted by a Thomas Myler who sent him to the famous St Paul's School in London where he made the acquaintance of boys – Antony Denny, Thomas Wriothesley and Edward North – who later became high officials in Henry VIII's court. He then went on to Cambridge and was admitted BA in 1522. He then entered the Lambeth household of Thomas Howard, Duke of Norfolk, as tutor to his son. After a short spell at Oxford he went to Paris where he studied Latin poetry and ancient manuscripts. He returned to England in 1529 and with the support of Cardinal Wolsey – Henry VIII's Chancellor – he became a royal chaplain. After the fall of Wolsey he approached his successor, Thomas Cromwell, as a patron. By 1533 he held four church benefices which gave him a comfortable income. Shortly afterwards he was given a commission by the King to search the libraries of monasteries and colleges in England and Wales and make a book-list of manuscripts prior to Cromwell's plan to 'dissolve' the monasteries. His first official journey was made to the West Country in 1533 and he was also engaged in refitting the King's libraries at Greenwich, Richmond and Westminster to receive monastic books.

After the 'dissolution' of the monasteries in 1536 he continued to search out books but also started to travel in search of history and topography with the intention of producing a map of England and Wales. In 1536 this exploration led to a series of journeys through every county in England and Wales and lasted until 1546. He kept detailed notes of his journeys but gave no exact account of the dates, the precise routes taken or the places where he stayed. He travelled on horseback and must have been accompanied by a travelling companion and had the help of local guides. His first itinerary was in Wales which took place in the summer seasons of 1536-9. It is likely that he had a prepared list of families who had given support to Henry VII at the Battle of Bosworth fifty years earlier. In addition Leland would have known the churches where he could stay. The notes written about northern Wales are disjointed and he

'In Anglesey it is now the practice to dig stony hillocks in their fields and with the stones they build walls in Devonshire fashion.'
Near Church Bay, Anglesey

SWTAN – the last thatched cottage in Anglesey – now National Trust.
Field walls – random dry stone collected from fields and beach.

had difficulty in understanding Welsh place names. It is, however, possible to reconstruct a coherent journey from the Shropshire border where he entered Maelor Saesneg and continued westwards to Llŷn. He gives lists of houses and their owners so that it is possible – by adding churches, castles, towns as well as rivers and coastal features – to indicate his route fairly accurately. He also refers to distances between places, directions, the course of rivers. He refers to mileages, furlongs and for short distances *'bow-shots'* which he intended at a later date to be used to produce maps. These rough notes were not intended for publication or as a literary effort. He refers to scenery, buildings, land-use especially woodland, and was keenly interested in local history and archaeology. Meeting a Mr Rowland Griffith at Penrhyndeudraeth he found someone who had detailed knowledge about the area. As they both looked southwards along the coast of Bae Ceredigion Rowland Griffith related the story of the drowning of Cartref Gwaelod which had been a fertile coastal plain between Tywyn and Aberdyfi *'In times past the plain had plenty of corn and grass but, being low-lying and almost level ground, the sea had many years ago inundated the land and it is now a sandy waste'.*

Rowland Griffith lived in Anglesey and *'at the church where he lived it was well-known that there was in ancient times a house of religion'.*

Also in Anglesey *'in time of mind'* the farmers did not separate their land but now a common practice is to *'dig stony hillocks in their fields and with the stones they build walls in Devonshire fashion'.*

In this process they *'dig up in many places earthenware pots with their mouths turned downwards and they contain human ash and bones'.*

Written at a time when archaeology as a subject did not exist and there was little concept of a period before the Romans, this is one of the earliest references to the ritual of cremation and the placing of bone and ash in inverted pots during the Bronze Age. Also in the *'depths of Anglesey where they dig peat they find great roots of trees that they use as wood. After the trees had been cut down earth and moss covered them and now with the removal of the overlying soil the old roots reappear."*

This was a reference to the submerged forest which is found along the northern and West coast of Wales and also attributed to a rise in sea level in the Bronze Age.

Information such as this greatly interested Leland but he reserved his main concern for towns and was a superb urban historian. His best descriptions are of the English market towns such as Malmesbury and

Ludlow. Unfortunately there were few towns in northern Wales. His finest description is of Denbigh which at the time of Leland's visit was undergoing rapid development outside the medieval walls below the castle. In northern Wales he concentrated on the physical landscape and even though he did not venture into Snowdonia he managed to record many of the lakes in a neat geographical context. His notes are based on observation and careful enquiry and give a marvellous account of northern Wales at the end of the Middle Ages.

'A NEW YEAR'S GIFT' (1546)

John Leland's 'Itinerary' of England and Wales

On the first of January 1546 John Leland presented Henry VIII with a 'New Year's Gift' which was a written report based on journeys throughout England and Wales which started in Wales in 1536. It was in investigation into the books and manuscripts to be found in monasteries and cathedrals; his resulting notebooks are an incomparable historical document of early Tudor England and Wales. His aim was wider than collecting manuscripts and became a lengthy visit to all the counties so that '. . . *there is almost neither cape nor bay, haven, creek or pier, rivers or confluence of rivers, beaches, lakes, meres, fens, mountain, moor, heather, forest, cities, castles, manors, monasteries, colleges but I have seen them'.*

Although this statement was an exaggeration he produced a comprehensive geographical survey without having any maps to help him. Leland was armed with the King's warrant; like Christopher Saxton, a few years later, who produced the first maps of the counties of England and Wales, was given the Queen's (Elizabeth I) warrant to travel and visit all areas of the country and people in authority were asked to *'give him all the help you can'*. His notebooks were intended for his personal use which he intended to fill in later so that there are gaps in the notes. Parts of the manuscript were damaged but fortunately a short while after Leland's death (1552) the London antiquarian, John Stow, copied the manuscript (in 1576) and both are now in the Bodleian Library, Oxford.

In his dedication to Henry VIII Leland said that he *'had conserved many good authors which otherwise had been like to have perished; of which in part remain in the most magnificent of your Royal Palaces'.*

John Leland had been the King's Librarian since 1530 and with his interest in Antiquities as well as books was well suited to visiting the libraries in cathedrals – such as the Chained Library at Hereford – and the monasteries. It was a critical time because the King's chief minister in 1534 was Thomas Cromwell who wanted to make the King, who had become head of the English Church after the break-up with Rome, *'the richest man that ever was'*. Towards fulfilling this aim Cromwell in 1535 had made a survey of all the churches and monasteries of England and Wales to discover their possessions, wealth and any abuses which could be levelled against them. A body of commissioners visited the monasteries and advised on their dissolution and the sale of their resources – gold, silver plate, ornaments, books – as well as their building materials and estates. Henry was anxious to preserve books and manuscripts and commissioned his Librarian, John Leland, to *'peruse and diligently search out all the libraries belonging to the religious houses, to make a survey of the books and manuscripts and find texts that would emphasise the supremacy of the King in his contest with Rome'.*

Leland, then aged thirty-three, had become the King's Antiquarian and in 1536 embarked on his mission to visit all counties of England and Wales. In his extensive travels he made detailed notes on the areas he visited as an important Royal official with the King's warrant. He visited Wales during the summers of 1536-39 just after the Act of Union between England and Wales (1536). He refers to the *'New Act'* which shows his journeys to have started in 1536. His reference to 'Flintshire lying north of Moldsdale' shows that his visit to northern Wales took place before 1541 when Moldsdale was added to Flintshire. He used official information about boundaries of lordships and commotes (districts) as well as bridges and roads – where they existed – houses and names of the local gentry who could provide accommodation. At that time there were only three knights with connections with the Royal household who were listed in northern Wales which reflected the relatively low proportion of rich landowners and two of these – Sir Roger Puleston and Sir John Hanmer – lived on the English Border in Maelor Saesneg. The chief landowner was Sir Roger Puleston who lived at Emral in Worthenbury and had served with Charles Brandon who was one of Henry VIII's greatest friends and was made Earl of Suffolk. Puleston had served with Brandon in his campaign in France in 1513. This gave Puleston, who was descended from an old Norman family, admittance to the Royal Household. Another knight, Sir William Griffith of Penrhyn near Bangor, had also served under Brandon in France and as a reward was granted the Chamberlainship of Caernarfonshire for life by Henry VIII.

There were many other lesser gentry of Welsh descent who had supported Henry VIII's father at the Battle of Bosworth. Rhys ap Maredudd of Plas Iolyn had been standard bearer at Bosworth and was rewarded with land. Later in the time of Henry VIII his sons were granted land from the dissolved monastic grange – Tir yr Abad – and built houses around Pentre Foelas. One of his sons, Robert, was chaplain to Cardinal Wolsey, Chancellor of Henry VIII before Cromwell. Another son Ellis

Price became a Commissioner who was directly involved in events leading to the Dissolution of the Monasteries and became a big landowner with a mansion or plas – Plas Iolyn near Pentrefoelas. Leland did not visit this remote part of Denbighshire but refers to the area as *'very barren but for oats grown with great labour. There is no wood, only peat, and it is full of hills and bogs.'*

Large areas of rough grass, marsh and peat bog and few trees are still a feature of this upland basin between Pentrefoelas and Cerrigydrudion (*'Kerreg Edridion'* according to Leland). Access through narrow gorges and dense forest from the Conwy valley around Llanrwst would have been difficult and would have deterred Leland.

Even in the western parts of Caernarfonshire there were many landowners who had supported Henry VII at Bosworth and had links with the Royal court. These houses were sufficiently well-spaced for Leland, travelling about ten miles a day on horseback, to cover northern Wales in reasonable comfort and safety with people who had given their loyalty to the King. As a gesture of thanks Leland gives the names of the houses and their owners so that his notebooks are a valuable source of local history, although most of the houses were shortly afterwards rebuilt or extended beyond recognition. Even so it was not possible to visit all parts of northern Wales because of inadequate roads and, in some areas, the local gentry could not guarantee Leland's safety.

One of the main areas to be avoided was the upper Dyfi valley around Dinas Mawddwy and Mallwyd. In this area the *'Gwylliaid Cochion Mawddwy'* – the Red Bandits of Mawddwy – held sway outside the law until the 1550s and Leland's only comment is to record *'Mawddwy'* as a commote in Meirionnydd and he had no interest or intention to visit the area; the nearest place he reached was Dolgellau. He also avoided another remote area – the upper Conwy Valley around Ysbyty Ifan where only ten years before Leland's time the bandits had been brought under control by a local warlord – Maredudd ap Ieuan who lived in Dolwyddelan Castle. In the peaceful aftermath his son, John Wynn ap Maredudd, settled further down the valley at Gwydir and was one of the 'new' men who were willing to give Leland a warm welcome. It was men such as John Wynn ap Maredudd who had detailed knowledge of the mountains and were able to give Leland information and help him make a detailed and accurate list of the main lakes of Snowdonia. These lists are a remarkable inventory at the time when people did not climb the high mountains and had no interest in their names or heights. The only mountain named and recognised was Snowdon which, even later, in the reign of Queen Elizabeth, was thought to be lower than Cader Idris.

Leland presented his 'New Year's Gift' on 1st January 1546 to the King but Henry's health grew steadily worse during the course of the year and he was not able to appreciate or understand the value of this remarkable 'Itinerary'.

'A New Year's Gift' was edited by J. Bale and published in 1549 under the title:

'THE LABORIOUS JOURNEY AND SEARCH OF JOHN LELAND FOR ENGLAND'S ANTIQUITIES'

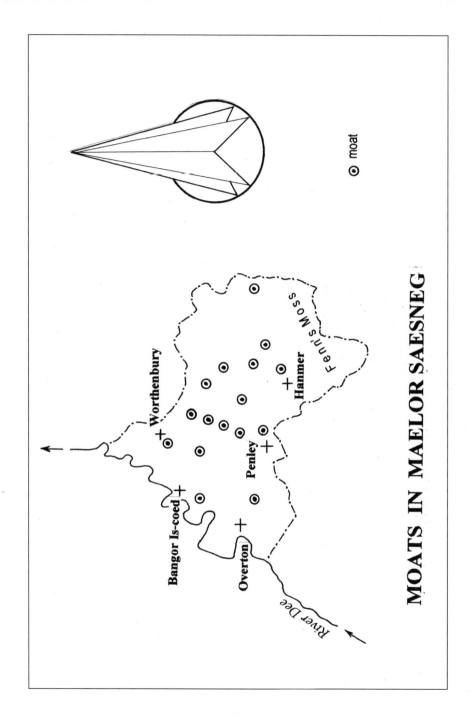

MOATS IN MAELOR SAESNEG

⊙ moat

Worthenbury

Hanmer

Fenn's Moss

Penley

Bangor Is-coed

Overton

River Dee

LAND OF MANOR-HOUSES AND MOATS

Maelor Saesneg

When Leland crossed the Border into Wales he would not have been aware of much change in the landscape in Maelor Saesneg (*English Maelor*) east of the river Dee. It was a land of farmers and lesser gentry with a scattering of manor houses many of which were enclosed by water-filled moats. Some of the houses have been demolished but many moats have survived and are shown on the O.S. maps. Maelor Saesneg has the largest concentration of moats in northern Wales and Leland's reference to 'Every gentleman has (in Hanmer parish) his attractive pools' may be a comment on the frequency of moated settlements.

The moats were dug – sometime in the 14th – 15th centuries – in the clays where flat land provided sites for timber-framed houses in areas where the extensive forests of Overton and Hanmer were cleared. Dug to a depth of six to twelve feet in the impervious clays which provided a stable bank, the moat surrounded the enclosed dry site for a house. The house was then built in the new 'island' and a wooden bridge would be used to cross the moat to the fields beyond.

The moat was not intended for defence and apart from its 'statement' as a status symbol it would be a valuable source of domestic water, fowl, fish and water for livestock. The water would also be a useful asset in coping with fires. Rainfall, run-off, seepage from ground water and springs were sufficient to keep the moats filled but sometimes brooks were diverted. At Emral Hall the Emral Brook formed the eastern side of the moat. The close-knit local families of the gentry – Pulestons, Hanmers, Dymocks, Broughtons and ap Richards – provided a 'culture' in which moat-building became the norm. It is interesting that when some of the families moved, on marriage, into the neighbouring district – across the Dee – of Maelor Gymraeg the moat-building also spread. Two manor houses – at Llay Hall and Lower Berse – were settled by the Pulestons of Emral Hall and both had moats – the moat at Llay Hall still survives In view of their vulnerability to changes in land use it is surprising that they have survived. One of the finest moats which has survived – apart from some filling in – is at New Hall, Chirk. It is spring- and stream-fed with fresh water filling the well-tended banks and a stone bridge giving access across the moat. If Leland visited New Hall – which he mentioned in

Aerial view of Halghton Moat.
Ridge-and-furrow field patterns cross the site (now dry) and are of later date.
© Clwyd Powys Archaeological Trust

Lightwood Farm Moat
Medieval ridge-and-furrow fields can be seen surrounding moat site.
© Clwyd Powys Archaeological Trust

1536-9 – he would be pleasantly surprised by the survival of the medieval moat which has become an attractive feature of the gardens.

The three parishes of Bangor, Overton and Hanmer which formed Maelor Saesneg were praised for their dense woodland, good crops of corn with pasture and meadow. The only drawback was the extensive peat bog which Leland called the 'Fennes' which is now known as 'Fenn's Moss' and the flooding of the Dee. Flooding in the past had destroyed Overton Castle and the medieval abbey at Bangor. However the area was dotted with hall-houses which Leland recorded and the names of their owners in 1536-9:

ALTHREY HALL Elis ap Richard
HANMER HALL Sir John Hanmer
EMRAL HALL   Sir Roger Puleston
LIGHTWOOD HALL* Edward Puleston
HALGHTON HALL   Dymock
BROUGHTON HALL Broughton

(* This was called 'COITEGOLLE' by Leland, which was his version of 'Coed Goleu' which means 'Lightwood Hall'.)

These were hall-houses which consisted mainly of a large open hall with the fire set in the hearth in the centre of the floor. The smoke escaped through a vent in the roof. The roof beams would be exposed and cut into elaborate designs – cusps, bosses and mouldings. At one end of the hall there would be a wooden screen separating the hall from the kitchen and buttery. At the other end the floor would be raised to form a dais on which the high table stood with a canopy above to prevent soot descending from the smoke-blackened rafters.

Most of the houses were drastically rebuilt after Leland's visit but one house – Althrey Hall – has survived after a vital rescue and magnificent restoration. By the 1980s the house had become ruinous and was bought by Tom Smith in 1986 who was a carpenter by trade and gifted in the art of restoring timber-framed houses. The building was based on timber frames of massive local oak from the adjoining Royal Forest of Overton. Oak beams up to 36 feet long and unjointed provided the basic frame. It had been built originally as a hall-house but by the time of Leland's visit an upper storey had been built, separate bedrooms divided by wattle and daub partitions were in place. An astonishing link with Leland's visit was

New Hall, Chirk
Section of the Moat. Wall in centre is the side of the bridge over the Moat
House – 18th century but remains of Tudor House in centre (behind bush).

made by Tom Smith when he discovered a wall-painting of Elis ap Richard and his wife Jane, who was a daughter of the Hanmers. It was found behind a wooden panel which had preserved it after it was painted in 1529/1530 just before Leland's visit to what he described as *'Elis ap Richard dwelleth yn Bangor at Althrey on Dee south syde, a fair house'*.

The painting was in colour using earth oxides, ochres and charcoal. It shows a man and woman in contemporary dress and had been done on dry plaster covering a partition wall of wattle and daub. In an adjoining room the name 'Richmond' scrawled on the wall referred to the Earl of Richmond who became Henry VII after the Battle of Bosworth (1485). This royal connection showed the support given to Henry VII at Bosworth by the then owner of Althrey – Richard ap Howell – who was rewarded with the King's sword and belt. The portrait shown was that of his son, Elis ap Richard, who inherited the house and welcomed Leland in 1536. Apart from this portrait there are other wall-paintings in three rooms including

Fenn's Moss
Peat digging 1973

the chapel on an upper storey which features a decorated ceiling with sun and moon symbols and an inscription, *IHS. NRI.* These paintings survived the defacement of 'idols' which proceeded later in the 16th century.

'HOLT IS A PLEASANT, RICH WELSH TOWN'

After leaving Bangor-on-Dee Leland crossed the River Dee and proceeded northwards to Holt which was then *'a pleasant rich Welsh town, governed by a mayor, having a fair once a year but the market is not as important as it was. It has an attractive church and a good castle.'*

Holt had been established as a borough centred around its castle on a sandstone hill overlooking the River Dee. Built after the Conquest of Wales (1284) the castle and town were granted to John de Warenne who became lord of Bromfield and Yale. The castle was built on a red sandstone outcrop which was quarried and the stone cut on the spot with the quarried area forming the moat around the new castle with water flowing in from the Dee. It had five sides with three-storeyed towers at each angle linked by a strong curtain wall. The entrance from the north-east was guarded by a square tower with a bridge over the moat leading into the inner courtyard. As Leland says it was *'a goodly castle'* and a prestigious residence and fit for a royal visitor. From the castle the affairs of Bromfield and Yale were administered

Holt Castle
Sited on an outcrop of red sandstone – also quarried locally and dressed stone used for walls and doorway of one of the corner towers.

with the records and revenues dealt with and stored in the gatehouse's Exchequer Tower.

The town was laid out in burgage plots north of the castle, the church (St Chad's) was built and a stone arched bridge across the Dee before Leland's visit which 'divides Cheshire from Bromfield'.

The town centre was an open space in front of the Court House where the mayor presided over the court sessions held every three weeks. In the open space an octagonal market cross was in place around which the burgesses would conduct their business, an annual fair

Holt, Market Cross

was held and the weekly market held on Fridays. On the steps of the market cross proclamations were made and announcements issued at a time when the population was illiterate. Like most buildings in Holt the cross was built of local red sandstone and had six steps leading to the base of an eight-foot high pinnacle.

The main building in the town was the fine medieval church (built 1240-1360) of St Chad's. It had been enlarged by Sir William Stanley before Leland's visit and had a font (1493) carved with the 24 heraldic symbols including the hart (stag) of Sir William who was then Constable of Holt Castle. Leland was impressed and described it as an *'attractive church'*.

St Chad's Church, Holt

St Chad's Church, Holt.
Leland would have been impressed by the font carved (1493) with 24 heraldic symbols
including the hart (stag) of Sir William Stanley. Constable of Holt Castle.

A SERJEANT-AT-ARMS AND A KING'S BODYGUARD

Leland in Bromfield

Leland crossed the River Dee – probably at Bangor – into the Lordship of Bromfield which was then administered from Holt. Holt was established by Edward I after the Statute of Rhuddlan (1284) and his appointee, John de Warenne, built a substantial castle on a sandstone hill overlooking the Dee. All that remains now is the outcrop and stone remnants but in Leland's day it was a fine castle with five towers and elegant apartments for the lord who was then the wealthy Sir William Stanley. Stanley was rewarded with land at Holt and Chirk for his support at the Battle of Bosworth and Henry VII had visited Holt Castle. The bridge also gave it importance but although by 1536 its annual fair was still held the market had ceased and its future mayoral status was in doubt. The church had been refurbished by Stanley in the late 15th century with wider aisles, extensions and windows but was subordinate to Gresford Church which was *'as fair a church as Wrexham having a steeple of 7 score feet with four pinnacled towers'* and which was also endowed by the Stanleys. Wrexham Church attracted Leland's attention as one of the finest in northern Wales as befitted the only market town in northern Wales with merchants and buckler (shield) makers. On his way from Gresford to Wrexham Leland passed, and perhaps visited, Llay Hall where *'Puleston, the knight, has a fair manor house in Gresford parish in Llay by marriage to a daughter and heir to the Hanmer family.'*

This manor house still survives with its massive chimneys and its surrounding moat is still partly intact and part of the garden. On his route south-westwards from Wrexham he passed and probably visited another Puleston house now called Lower Berse farm. Here Leland refers to *'John Puleston, serjeant-at-arms, has a manor house and place within half a mile of Wrexham at Marsche'*.

At this time Lower Berse was known as 'PLAS YM MERS' which Leland transcribed as 'MARSCHE' perhaps mistaking a Welsh pronunciation!

John Puleston had inherited the Plas ym Mers estate from his father who had served Henry VII at Bosworth field (1488) and had been

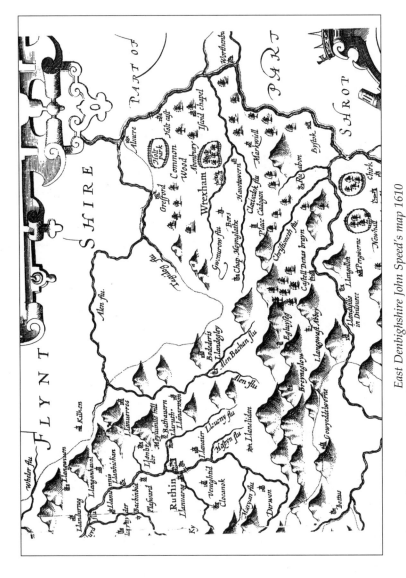

East Denbighshire John Speed's map 1610

shows Leland's route: Holt – Gresford – Wrexham – Berse – Ruabon – New Hall – Chirk – Llangollen –
Valle Crucis (Llanegwystl Abbey) – Llandegla – Llanarmon – Llanferres

rewarded with an annuity of 20 marks (£13.6s.8d), was an usher at the King's Court and later became Constable of Caernarfon Castle. John Puleston became Henry VIII's Serjeant-at-arms and by Leland's visit was a trusted royal servant and would have given Leland a great welcome. The old house may have had a moat and was rebuilt in 1873 but part of the old house was preserved and incorporated in the new building. The huge stone building with its massive chimney, its large fireplace, kitchen and former cheese-room has survived from Leland's time.

The whole of Bromfield was rich in corn and pasture and, especially in Ruabon parish, woodland. Leland mentions 'John Eyton lives in Ruabon' and *'the river Abon passes the Ruabon church wall and after running less than a mile joins the Dee'.*

It is possible that Leland then entered the Lordship of Chirk, south of Ruabon, where the two most important gentlemen were *'Trevor dwells in Chirk parish at Plas Newydd, Edwards' son dwells not far from Chirk Castle'.*

The Edwards family had resided for many years at Plas Newydd having moved from their old house at Pengwern in an abandoned loop of the River Dee east of Llangollen. Like other well-known families they had supported Henry VII at Bosworth and in 1513 William Edwards had taken part in the Battle of Tournai in France in Henry VIII's army. He was rewarded with the office of Constable of Chirk Castle, near Plas Newydd, and also a member of the Royal Household as King's bodyguard and Serjeant of the Pantry. William Edwards' son John – referred to by Leland – lived in a fine mansion at Plas Newydd surrounded by a large moat the sides of which faced the cardinal points with the west side 57 yards long and the north side 69 yards which were sufficient to enclose a large house with a bridge across the moat. It is likely that they drew the necessary workmen and skills from Maelor Saesneg where they held land. Much of this medieval moat survives on the south side with a stone bridge almost as Leland saw it. The house was acquired by the Myddeltons of Chirk Castle in 1721 and they built a fine Georgian house in the 1740s on the old site. The house had changed its name to 'New Hall' – a translation of 'Plas Newydd' – in Elizabethan times as is shown on John Speed's map (1611). A small building attached to the New Hall has an arched Tudor doorway and inside a low beam over a large, step-in fireplace with carved overmantle which are the remnants of the old Tudor house.

Thus in passing through Bromfield on his way to Llangollen and Valle Crucis Leland would have been given a great welcome and safe passage by the Pulestons, Eytons, Edwardses and Trefors who were trusted Royal servants with some serving in the King's Household.

Llay Hall
Remains of the medieval moat. The hall-house has fine aisle-trusses.

Plas ym Mers (now Lower Berse)
Remnant of the old house – stone – contrasting with the late 19th century brick wings.

'THE RIVER COMES BY RUABON CHURCH WALL'

An Effigy and Wall Painting in Ruabon Church

On his way from Wrexham through Bromfield to Valle Crucis Leland passed through Ruabon and gives an eye-witness account of *'the river comes by Ruabon Church Wall'*.

He refers to the large extent of Ruabon parish which had the best woodland in Bromfield and *'a good quarry of grinding stones'*.

He may have stayed near Ruabon because he refers to John Eyton who *'lives in Ruabon'*.

At this time the replacement of a surname in the English style for the old Welsh 'ap' (son of) distinguished John Eyton from his father – John ap Elis Eyton – who had died a few years earlier in 1526. John Eyton may have taken Leland into the church to see the newly-installed effigy in alabaster to his father and mother. Entering the church they would have been impressed by the effigy – one of the finest in Wales – of two figures lying in medieval style on a tomb-chest with hands in prayer and with a Latin inscription for the reader to 'pray for the souls of John ap Elis Eyton (d. 1526) and his wife Elizabeth (d. 1524)'. John ap Elis Eyton had taken part in the Battle of Bosworth (1485) in support of Henry VII who rewarded him with large estates around Ruabon and an annuity of 10 marks. The alabaster effigy was probably carved at Burton-on-Trent where the finest craftsmen had their workshops and the gypsum deposits were found. The effigy shows a medieval knight in armour with helmet and an S.S. collar which was the livery of members of the Lancastrians who brought Henry VII to the throne. His gauntlets were placed at his side and were leather covered with steel plates. Elizabeth was dressed in a long dress of a lady of the early 16th century. The finely carved effigies were a mark of wealth and status and would have interested Leland who was on a mission to visit families who had helped to establish the Tudor dynasty. He was visiting the first-generation descendants of the men who had taken part in the Battle of Bosworth and Leland had a list of their names.

Also in the church at the time of Leland's visit was the fine medieval wall-painting dating to the first half of the 15th century. Most churches in the Middle Ages had wall-paintings which were used for teaching purposes in an illiterate society to enlighten the congregations with Biblical texts and stories. The painting on the south wall of the church was probably applied before the plaster was dry and was a fresco similar to those found in Italian churches. The powdered pigments were mainly red, yellow and brown obtained from ferric oxide and ochres. The theme at Ruabon was the Acts of Mercy including feeding the hungry, giving drink to the thirsty, clothing the naked and receiving strangers. Each person is shown performing his or her act of mercy and a rare feature is the depiction of a woman

Ruabon Church – wall painting shows one of the Biblical scenes namely, giving drink to the thirsty. A rare feature is the depiction of a woman who was dressed in the style of the early 15th century.

who was dressed in the style of the early 15th century. They were inspired by angels and the morality subjects were based on a text from St Matthew's Gospel (XXV). The form, character and expression of the figures are excellently drawn, the colours are vivid and make the painting one of the finest in Wales. Although Henry VIII had removed the Pope's authority over the English church in the 1530s the Sunday services at all the parish churches were still Catholic in ritual, and Latin in liturgy; statues and paintings were also still unaltered. It was not until 1547 that edicts were enforced banning and removing images and statues and all wall paintings were to be covered with layers of whitewash. It was the removal of these layers of plaster and whitewash during the restoration of the church in 1870 which led to the discovery of the wall painting. An early 15th century date was inferred from the style of costumes and was confirmed by the verse in Welsh to explain the meaning of the painting:

And the seven deeds (expected of) the believers
Which should all be performed for the sake of the weak;
Supply food and drink when they come seeking,
Attend to the suffering of invalids,
Carry the dead from the hill to the church,
Befriend every jailed prisoner,
Give board and lodgings to those in need of shelter,
And clothing against the elements.

This was written by the priest at Ruabon (in 1430) – Maredudd ap Rhys –and was added to the mural after its discovery in 1870.

Ruabon Church
Alabaster effigy of John ap Elis Eyton (d.1526)
and wife Elizabeth on a tomb-chest.

43

'THIS BOOK BELONGS
TO THE ABBEY AT VALLE CRUCIS'

Valle Crucis

Leland mentions Valle Crucis but only to give its position – half a mile from the River Dee – in Yale commote (Iâl). He also mentions good crops of corn with meadow and pasture around the abbey for cattle and sheep. The steep sides of the valley were clothed in dense forest in contrast to the rocky slopes and treeless mountains of Yale where the people burned peat rather than wood. He avoided a description of the abbey itself and yet he was there at the time when the dissolution or breaking up of the abbey (1536-7) was in progress. By January 1537 the monks had been evicted and the sale of moveable items was taking place. Valuable materials such as the bells and silver plate were taken to London to be sold and melted down. Lead, originally from nearby Minera, taken from the roof was smelted on the spot. All of the interior furnishings – glass, tiles, altar tables, vestments, doors – were auctioned on the spot in the Chapter House. Many of the manuscripts from the small library were probably sold off for their value as parchment or vellum, but fortunately two priceless manuscripts survived, probably carried away secretly before the dissolution because one manuscript has been in Eton since 1521.

A narrow chamber in the thickness of the wall of the Chapter House fronting the Cloister Walk was the book-cupboard or library of the abbey. At least two books have survived and would have been vital and compulsory reading in the Chapter House. Both were important in the daily readings by one of the monks. The older manuscript incredibly dates to the foundation of the abbey (1201) and appropriately records the life of St Bernard of Clairvaux who expanded the Cistercian Order which aimed at founding abbeys *far from the haunts of men*, which would have been a good description of their new site at Valle Crucis. The book would have been a valuable reminder of the aims of the Order and is now in the Bodleian Library, Oxford, where its first page in a 13th century hand clearly reads:

LIBER SANCTE MARIA DE VALLE CRUCIS
LIBRARY OF ST MARY OF VALLE CRUCIS

Library or Book-cupboard (left) with elaborately decorated screen in the thickness of the west wall of the Chapler House (centre – arched doorway). Had its own entrance with large windows on each side. On right, small pointed door opens on to narrow staircase in the thickness of the wall – leading to the monks' dormitory.

Valle Crucis abbey with the ruins of Dinas Brân (on the hill-top) – one of the castles of northern Powys. Madog ap Gruffudd Maelor founded the abbey on 28th January, 1201.

Leland records that Dinas Brân was never a large castle but was sited on a strong hill-top position almost inaccessible to enemies. 'It is now entirely ruined' 1536.

Interior of the Chapter House where the monks each morning gathered to listen to a chapter of their Rule. Dressed stone pillars – four – which supported the weight of the vaulted ribs forming the roof. Windows – with elaborate tracery – faced east and caught the morning sunlight. A square room.

since all Cistercian monasteries were dedicated to St Mary and the Latin script is perfectly preserved.

The other manuscript is later in date (15th century) and was also essential reading in the Chapter House. It contains the Dialogues of Pope Gregory the Great who wrote the life of St Benedict who established the rules of prayer, work and study for the earliest monasteries of Western Europe. Gregory sent Augustine, a monk in Rome, in 597 to convert the King of Kent to Christianity. King Aethelbert was converted and Augustine founded a monastery in Canterbury and in 601 became the first Archbishop of Canterbury. The manuscript at Valle Crucis, now in Eton, includes a work by St Augustine and its last page, a fading inscription in Latin, confirms that the manuscript or *'book belongs to the Abbey at Valle Crucis'*. Both books would have been magnificent treasures for the monks and a great effort must have been made to ensure their safety and survival.

Leland is clear in his evaluation of the economic life at Valle Crucis but is silent on its dissolution and future. Perhaps it was too controversial a subject to be raised by a Royal official; in 1537 it had been sold to Sir William Pickering and was undergoing demolition at the time of his Itinerary.

'THE RIVER THAT BECOMES DRY'

Leland's Itinerary – Valle Crucis To Mold

From Valle Crucis we can trace with some confidence Leland's route to Yale (Iâl) because of the exact detail and the correct sequence of places named. He followed the steep slopes of the Oernant Pass from the flat meadows of the abbey reaching the summit at just over 1300 feet. On the north side of the pass he passed close (perhaps visited) the Abbot's summer house (Hafod yr Abad) where the lay-brothers tended large flocks of sheep on the hill pastures. At Hafod yr Abad today – still a large sheep farm – there is a curious survival which may be a direct link with the abbey. This is a stoup or shallow stone basin projecting from the thick walls inside the house which contained 'holy' water. When visitors entered the house they would dip their fingers in the water and make a sign of the cross. The stoup would have been made by stone masons at the abbey who were used to cutting sepulchral slabs and gravestones. The stoup usually found near the entrance door or porch of a church has a moulded edge and the small drainage hole still shows its original function.

A short distance below Hafod yr Abad, Leland noticed *'Llin Alen'* which he identified as the exact source of the River Alun which he noted was *'the greatest water beside the Dee that is in any part of Yale'*.

To call it a *'llyn'* (lake) is an exaggeration and it would be more suitable to call it a pool. It was situated just below the track – now the A542 – at Plas y Bwlch farm and this pool since Leland's time has been reduced in size by drainage and building work. Leland does not clearly distinguish between a lake and pool; in Snowdonia Llyn Anafon is described as a *'little pool'*. However its site is still existing and it gives a year-round water supply to the Alun. It flows out as a small brook and according to Leland flows *'from west to east first to Llandegla'*.

By the time it reaches Llandegla it has become a small river needing bridge crossings; it passes St Tegla's well – which feeds the Alun – and then runs just below the hillside church at Llandegla. The well was famous in Leland's day attracting many visitors who made substantial offerings. A typical annual offering was over £2.13s. and the mention refers to gold nobles. The well had a reputation for curing epilepsy which was one of the most feared diseases of the Middle Ages. During the

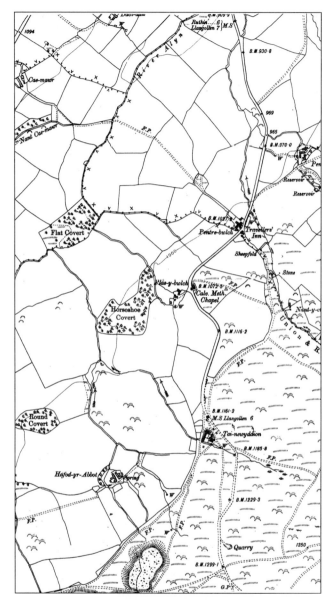

O.S. Map 1914
Hafod yr Abad (bottom left)
'Llin Alen' – the source of the River Alun – mentioned by Leland
– ¼" West of W (well) of Plâs yn Bwlch in the centre of the map.

excavation of the well in 1938 pottery, pins and coins were found. Strangely although Leland mentions Llandegla as a *'famous parish'* but he ignores Tegla's well. However he does mention 'John Llued dwellith in Llandegla parish' which is a reference to John Lloyd who lived in a tower-like fortified house at Bodidris east of the village. He was a descendant of Llywelyn ap Ynyr, a medieval soldier who served the Prince of Powys at the battle of Crogen (1165) against Henry II. Llywelyn was rewarded with land at Llanarmon – at Gelligynan. His son Gruffudd ap Llywelyn consolidated the estate and is depicted as a medieval knight in armour (c.1320) in a fine effigy still surviving in Llanarmon church in the neighbouring parish adjoining Llandegla. By Leland's time the descendants of Gruffudd ap Llywelyn had been Llued or Lhuyd and later in the 16th century, Lloyd. The Lloyds held important estates at Gelligynan and Bodidris. As Leland followed the track alongside the Alun towards Llanarmon he also passed tracts of pasture belonging to Valle Crucis; these granges extended along the Alun from Hafod yr Abad, Buddugre'r Abad, Creigiog Grange and, just north of Llanarmon, Banhadlan. Lay-brothers worked these pastures which supported sheep and cattle.

When Leland reached Llanarmon he mentioned 'Edward Llued yn Llanarmon' who probably lived at Gelligynan and may have provided hospitality for this section of his journey. He may however have stayed at the old house which still stands just outside the churchyard at Llanarmon. This may have been the priest's house and is still referred to as the 'Old Vicarage'. Medieval wall paintings on the staircase are alleged to have existed and niches for holding crosses survive in the attic. Leland must have stayed in Llanarmon which was a day's horse ride from Valle Crucis and roughly half way from the abbey to Mold. Llanarmon with its medieval castle (Y Faerdre) was the 'capital' of Yale and its church had been extended in the years just before Leland's visit. He records that there had been *'a great pilgrimage and offering was of late to S. Armon'*.

According to the official investigation of church and monastic finances – Valor Ecclesiasticus – in 1535 the offering made to the image of St Garmon came to £4.10s. and would probably have been placed in the black-oak chest which now lies near the West Door. With increased prosperity at the end of the 15th century churches in the Vale of Clwyd and at Llanarmon were rebuilt and enlarged. The simple single-nave church was transformed by the building of another nave with the

Llanarmon Church
Effigy of Gruffudd ap Llywelyn – a medieval knight c.1320

St Tegla's Well, Llandegla. Well chamber (now in disrepair)
on left . . . spring flowing strongly to join River Alun.

Llanarmon-yn-Iâl Church

Bodidris Hall
Tower – (left-centre) was home of John Lloyd.

separating wall converted by finely moulded pillars and arches.

Leaving Llanarmon Leland continued to follow the River Alun through Llanferres parish and then into Moldsdale lordship at *'a place called Hespalen it runs into the ground by a space of a quarter of a mile'*.

This observation refers to a well-known feature of the river which in periods of reduced flow sinks through cracks and fissures in the limestone bed and then flows underground. Heavy rains in late summer or autumn increase its flow from its large catchment area and it resumes normal surface flow throughout the winter and spring. It is likely that Leland saw this in summer and was given information by a local guide. Once again it shows Leland's great interest in the river. When he reached Mold he describes the plan of the town – its castle, streets and houses – and had a reference to the Alun which *'comes within a bow-shot of Mold church'* and then there is (to the south of the town) *'another river called Afon Terrig almost as big as the Alun which flows into the Alun'*.

The river flows southwards through Hopedale – which was then part of Flintshire – into Bromfield and joins the Dee half a mile below Holt Bridge.

The details given of his journey from Valle Crucis to Mold accompanied by guides is a remarkable trek using tracks and keeping as near as possible to the River Alun. No maps were available and he would have encountered narrow gorges, steep slopes, difficult fording points and dense forests.

Survival of a medieval place-name: now farm Hafod yr Abad, summer pasture of the Abbot (of Valle Crucis Abbey)

* bow-shot – range of fire of a cross-bow (about 250 yards).

* Another summer-dry river is Nant Hafesp, 1 mile east of Bala, which flows through Llanfor village.

* Horseshoe Pass – a new pass built 1811 with a gentler gradient replaced steep pass north of Pentre Dwr.

* Double-nave churches are a common feature of the Vale of Clwyd with some extensions outside, e.g. Caerwys, Llanarmon-yn-Iâl.

52

'PLENTY OF WATER AND OTHER GOOD THINGS'

Moldsdale

The lordship of Moldsdale established after the Norman Conquest (1066), under the control of the Earl of Chester, was placed in the hands of Robert Montalt from whom the name Mold originates. He built a motte and bailey castle on a steep hill overlooking the River Alun. The last of the Montalt family died in 1329 and it became part of the Stanley (Earl of Derby) family estate. The present church was built on an older foundation in the late 15th century by the Stanleys who also built churches at Wrexham, Holt, Northop and Gresford. Before Leland's time (1536-9) there were no records dealing with Mold apart from a violent episode in 1465 when the Mayor of Chester visited the town with an armed gang. The mayor, Robert Byrne, was kidnapped by Rhinallt Griff ap Bleddyn who lived outside the town at the Tower, Broncoed, where he was hanged. Despite this rough justice Moldsdale under the Stanley regime at that time had town officials and the Court House at Mold is recorded. The lord of Moldsdale had the right to judge cases in Mold and Gwernymynydd, Nerquis, Treuddyn and Bistre according to local law and custom. Mold, by Leland's visit, had lost its market but two annual fairs were held. Many of the houses – of which in 1536 only forty were inhabited – were derelict or in very poor condition.

The main street – Bailey Street ('*Streate Byle*') – ran down the hill from the castle to intersect with Court House Street which in Welsh was called '*Streate Dadlede*' – the 'Street of Debate'. There were small lanes leading off these two main streets with small houses. By Leland's time the castle at the top end of Bailey Street was in ruins with only ditches and mounds and on the side of the hill '*a fayre spring*'.

The River Alun was a 'bow-shot' – about 250 yards – from the church but no bridge over the river was mentioned by Leland who usually recorded them if they existed. The southern limit of the town was marked by the line of a brook called '*Houne*' which flowed into the Alun river.

Most of Moldsdale was level ground which produced good quality corn. There were shallow coal pits three-quarters of a mile from the town. This was an area of outcrop coal near the Alun where even today pieces

Mold Church – built by Margaret Beaufort, wife of Sir William Stanley and referred to casually by Leland – 'The River Alun comes within a bow-shot of Mold Church'.

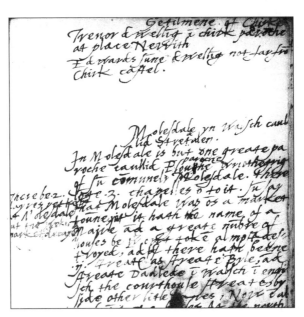

Molesdale (Moldsdale) from John Leland's notebook – in his own handwriting.
© Bodleian Library, Oxford

of coal are found in the gardens at Pentre.

There were three important houses in 1536-9 which were just outside the town:

1. Robert Edwards was a gentleman living at Rhual on the side of the River Alun with plenty of wood which was carted to Chester and he also had river meadows.
2. Ithel (or Ellis) Griffiths lived on the north side of Mold at Llwynegrin.
3. John Wynne ap Robert lived in a stone tower called Broncoed or Rhinallt's Tower three-quarters of a mile from the town. There was a small brook running near the Tower and flowing for a quarter of a mile to join the Alun.

Just to the south of the Tower there was a large river called Afon Terrig – almost as big as the Alun – which flowed from Yale and into Moldsdale to join the Alun. There were many small rills and brooks and with the numerous springs there was plenty of water in this five-mile long parish of Moldsdale and *'many other good things'* ' . . . *well servid of water and of dyvers other good thinges'*.

'THE LAST THROW OF THE MIDDLE AGES'

The Tower (Broncoed, Mold)

From the details given it seems likely that Leland visited and probably stayed at the Tower on his journey through Moldsdale. His usual reference to a house is brief – the names of the house and its owner at the time. In his reference to the Tower he gives plenty of detail:

> *'John Wenne ap Roberte dwells at a stone tower called Broncoit [Broncoed] or Regnault's Tower, three quarters of a mile from Mold. There is a small rill running near this square tower called _____ and a quarter of a mile beneath the tower joins the River Alun running from west to east.'*

This amount of careful observation and detail indicates a visit and probably a short stay here. In the previous century the builder of the tower (1445) was Rheinallt Gryf ap Bleddyn who supported the Lancastrian cause which in 1485 led to the accession of Henry VII, father of Henry VIII and patron of Leland. This would have been an added incentive to visit for Leland as well as the hospitality and security.

The house was built (1445) as a fortified tower in the style of a medieval castle with an attached building (hall or kitchen) and a cattle enclosure intended to withstand attack and siege. It was similar in design and function to the Pele towers of Cumbria. A famous incident in 1465 is recorded by Lewys Glyn Cothi. Involved in a fray with men from Chester visiting the fair at Mold, Rheinallt captured and later hanged a former major of Chester, Robert Byrne, and a retaliatory raid by citizens from Chester resulted in a battle at the Tower with many killed. Another contemporary poet, Hywel Cilan, describes it as *'Fair tower, a fortress 120 feet high but . . . with three tables, wine and also, on one side, a kitchen'.*

The tower in which Leland would have been welcomed is still intact with its stonework refaced and is one of the finest buildings from the Middle Ages in northern Wales. Entering from the main oak door there are spiral stairs to a small vaulted undercroft of uncertain purpose but was perhaps a dungeon. The ground floor above has a high vaulted ceiling and the spiral staircase in the thick walls leads to an elegant chamber above which there is access to a low-pitched roof behind a parapet and wall-walk. The Tower was built as a fortified house as a

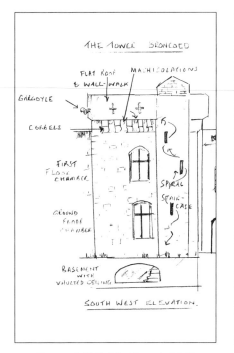

*Broncoed Hall (The Tower), Mold
Arrow-slits provide light for the
spiral staircase.*

The Tower, Broncoed

refuge of safety and security. At the roof level, as in a medieval castle, there are corbels which jut out from the walls to support the weight of the roof. Between the corbels there are holes (machicolations) for dropping stones or oil on any attackers from below. Grotesque gargoyles project from the corbel heads at the corners and add to the fearsome character of the building. The Tower is in such an excellent condition that Leland would recognise it as the one he visited in 1536-9 as 'a square stone tower' and would be pleased to know that the rill to the north is still running strongly eastwards to join the River Alun.

'MANY GO TO MARKET ON TUESDAYS'

Tudor Denbigh

Denbigh at the time of Leland's visit (1536-9) was one of the main towns in northern Wales and with its hill-top castle and its large garrison, its walled town and church was the subject of Leland's most memorable description. His detailed and exact account suggests that he was there as a royal official given hospitality and security by the Constable of the Castle. The town was then in an interesting stage because it had expanded outside the medieval walls and in 1536 had become the county town of the newly-created Denbighshire. It was also situated in the rich farming area of the Vale of Clwyd with a flourishing market where 'Many go to market on Tuesday'.

There was a castle on the site during the region of the welsh princes – it was held by Dafydd ap Gruffudd during the Welsh War of Independence, 1282. During Norman occupation, a new castle was built by Earl Lacy, who was rewarded by Edward I for his services in the war and a new English borough was set up around the Castle in the new Lordship of Denbigh. The main gate through the walls was Burgess Gate – which still stands – with two massive towers and a vaulted entrance passage guarded by three rows of murder holes in the roof and a strong new portcullis. Its name refers to its use by the burgesses who could attend public meetings independently of the castle. By Leland's visit many houses within the medieval walls had been demolished; less than eighty remained and by the end of the century most of the area was an empty space around the church. The church of St Hilary was a chapel of ease for the local inhabitants because the parish church of St Marcella was well outside the town. The walls were intact with another gate – the Exchequer Gate used by the Lord – three towers and the Goblin Tower standing outside the walls but which had lost its lead roof eighty years before as a result of a tempest. The castle itself was also in good condition with a massive gatehouse and, according to Leland, if the castle had been finished it would have been one of the most impressive in England (and Wales). On the front of the gate there was a stone 'image' of Lacy, Earl of Lincoln, in his stately robes, and prayers were said for him – over 200 years after his death – each Sunday at St Hilary's church.

By Leland's time the town outside was three times larger than the

Denbigh Friary 1742
by S. & N. Buck

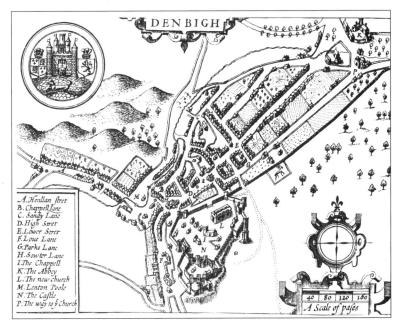

Denbigh
John Speed's map 1610

walled town. It ran from below Burgess Gate as a single High Street which was also the market square with its market cross. It then stretched down the steep hill to the flat meadow where the White Friars' Priory stood. One house standing today (32 High Street) was only built 30 years after Leland's visit and gives an idea of houses of the period. Some of the narrow lanes off High Street have also survived and include Sowter Lane.

Most of the buildings described by Leland were – only 70 years later – depicted in the plan of Denbigh drawn by John Speed (1610) and little had changed in the lay-out so it was almost exactly as Leland saw it in 1536-9. The castle is shown (N) with St Hilary's church marked as THE CHAPPELL (I). Just outside the walls was LOVE LANE (F) which was one of the oldest streets in Denbigh with some burgage-plot deeds dated 1444. HIGH STREET (D) is shown with a market cross standing in the centre of the market square. Narrow lanes such as SOWTER LANE (H) were lined with densely-packed terraced houses and CHAPPELL LANE (B) led downhill to LENTON POOLE (M) now Lenten Pool, which provided fish during Lent. The High Street gave way down the steep hill as LOWER STREET (E) which led to ABBEY (K) which was the White Friars' Priory. One important street – PARKE LANE (G) ran parallel to Lower Street and at (P) was the 'road to the church' (St Marcella's) outside the town limits. PARKE LANE was wide but had few houses which were mainly large and had gardens. The street bordered the Deer Park from which it was separated by a belt of pasture, crops and woodland. It would have been the most attractive part of the town in Tudor times. However it was colloquially known as 'Beggars Lane' from its use by the Mendicant Friars from the Priory to the castle who begged for alms for the poor.

The map, although drawn 70 years later, confirms all the information given by Leland; the main discrepancy is THE NEW CHURCH (L) which had been started in 1579 by Robert Dudley, Earl of Leicester. He was then the Lord of Denbigh and had the intention of transferring the Cathedral of St Asaph to Denbigh but the 'new church' was never completed. The road passing Lenten Pool leading to the village of Henllan – HENLLAN STREET (A) passed the Tudor plas of Foxhall where the 12-year old Humphrey Lhwyd lived (in 1536). After his education at Oxford University he, like Leland, became an antiquarian scholar and produced the first accurate map of Wales. For Leland himself it was a good time to visit Denbigh and he recorded a memorable description in his notebooks.

In Leland's day the towns of northern Wales were small in size and population with Wrexham, the largest, having only between 1,500-2,000 people. The castle-towns of Denbigh and Caernarfon had between 1,000 and 1,500 people but both were expanding outside the gates and medieval walls. Both towns were shown on John Speed's maps which were the first reasonably accurate town plans with named buildings, streets and even houses.

Denbigh Castle
St Hilary's Church – remains of the tower within the town walls.

Burgess Gate, Denbigh
This was the main entrance gate through the town walls. It had two massive towers and a vaulted entrance passage.
Murder holes in the roof and portcullis.

'A WORTHY, PLENTIFUL HOUSE'

Plas or Hall-House

One of Leland's commonest references is to *'place'* to describe a substantial house which in Welsh was denoted as a 'plas' built in the 15th and 16th centuries by the lesser gentry. They were built on good sites with fresh water, good building materials – in stone and timber – and with fertile land – corn, meadow, pasture and woodland. He records *'Place Newid'* (Plas Newydd) near Chirk and *'Place Penrine'* (now Penrhyn Old Hall) – *'an ancient stone house'* – both of which, although rebuilt later, have survived. He pays little attention to houses in the Vale of Clwyd but gives a detailed account of farming referring to corn-fields, pasture and meadow. The reason for the omission is probably due to the welcome he received at Denbigh Castle; he felt no obligation to name houses and their owners in the Vale. There were more plasdai in the Vale of Clwyd than anywhere else in northern Wales and this reflected its favourable soils,

Plas Uchaf near Llangollen
A typical half-timbered Tudor 'Plas'

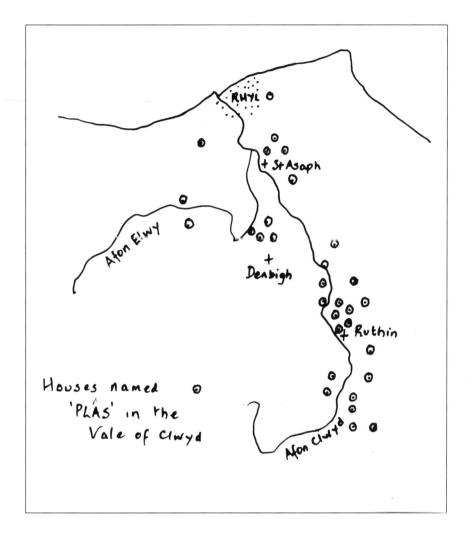

Houses named
'PLÂS' in the
Vale of Clwyd

water resources and climate – in its sheltered position under 30" of rain a
year and plenty of sunshine.

There were so many plasdai in the Vale of Clwyd that a 'surname' or
suffix was needed to distinguish them and the word 'plas' itself was a
much sought-after status symbol. In the lower areas 'isaf' was added to
distinguish it from a neighbouring 'uchaf' (upper). Proximity to a village
such as Plas Llanarmon and Plas Llanynys gave a clearly identified
location. In the Vale of Clwyd its two main building stones gave Plas Coch

(Red House) based on red sandstone to distinguish it from Plas Gwyn (White Hall) based on limestone. Plas Cefn suggested a hill or ridge-top position whereas Plas yn Rhos was a valley bottom site. A reference to the builder or occupant, as in Plas Clough near Denbigh, built by Sir Richard Clough, whereas Plas Esgob was the home of the Bishop. The local trees in area of woodland gave Plas Onn (ash) and Plas Bedw indicated a birch grove. The commonest place-name in northern Wales is Plas Newydd, which showed the owner's status and pride in building a 'new house'.

The Vale of Clwyd has the largest concentration of plasdai in northern Wales with thirty-one shown on the O.S. map. They also extend from the English border to the extreme west in Llŷn with Plas yn Rhiw a fine example overlooking Porth Neigwl (Hell's Mouth). Their sites, although chosen 400-500 years ago, show an uncanny perception of future geography which enabled them to prosper and survive. The finest example of all is Plas Mawr in Conwy which was built only a generation after Leland's visit and is considered the best preserved Elizabethan town house in Britain. It was modestly described by a contemporary as a *'Worthy, Plentiful House'*.

Penrhyn Old Hall

'AN ANCIENT STONE HOUSE
AND A PLEASANT PLACE'

Penrhyn Old Hall and Gwydir Castle

After his stay in Denbigh, Leland probably rode westwards towards the Conwy valley along the coast crossing Afon Gele near Abergele and then the Dulas Valley. Here the thick limestone beds outcropped above the river and further up the valley there were slaty mudstones. This was almost certainly his route because his notes are based on close observations rather than gathered information.

> 'There is a quarry of hard stone. It is a black or sad marble in colour much used for ovens and chimneys . . . and there they also dig out slate stones to cover their houses.'

This is a good contemporary account of the geology of the area (Llanddulas) at a time when the open hearth in the floor and the smoke-escape hole in the roof were being replaced by chimneys in the wall (often outside) and large fireplaces. Slate was replacing thatch in the new storeyed houses.

After the steep climb over the Leadland Penmaenrhos, he entered the commote of Creuddyn, which then belonged to Caernarfonshire and his reference to it being located *'this side of the Conwy river'* showed that he was travelling westwards. He noted that:

> 'This commote is partly by the Conwy River and partly by the sea made into an island and one way out of Denbighshire is over a man made causeway over the marsh which is often flooded.'

This is a perceptive description of this very flat area now called 'Morfa Penrhyn' and 'Morfa Rhyd'. The name 'Morfa' (sea-marsh) shows that at high tide it is prone to flooding in which case it would make Creuddyn an island. It is possible that the straight line of the B5115 is on the course of this medieval causeway to Penrhyn. Here:

'Plas Penrhyn, an ancient stone house east-north-east of the sea belongs to Mr Powell (of Flintshire).

This is now known as Penrhyn Old Hall but little survives of the 'ancient' house except the walls and footings of the south-west block because it was rebuilt shortly after his visit. The limestone rubble and the large corner stones are still visible and some square-headed first-floor windows were re-used. The best survival is the small tre-foil window which was re-set in a first floor room above the entrance door. It dates to the 15th century and belongs to the 'ancient house'. The medieval nail-studded oak door is also in fine condition and was also probably re-used. The coat of arms of Ednyfed Fychan, Seneschal of Llywelyn the Great, is a reminder that he had estates locally in Creuddyn. By the 1590s the house had been completely rebuilt and is now a fine example of an Elizabethan 'Plas'.

His onward visit westwards may have been delayed by a detour to visit Gwydir opposite Llanrwst and only a short distance – eight miles – along the river meadows of the Conwy. He probably rode past Maenan Abbey, then in the throes of demolition and crossed the River Conwy just below Llanrwst where it could be easily forded in summer. He found Gwydir an attractive house *'John Wynn ap Meredith lives at Gwydir. It is a pretty place.'*

The Wynns were an old family related to the Tudors and gave their full support to the Lancastrian cause before Henry VII's victory at Bosworth. John Wynn's father Maredudd (or Meredith) had also served Henry VIII in the siege of Tournai (1513) in France. After living at Dolwyddelan Castle he had moved down the river to Gwydir and had built a new house – a fortified manor-house – before his death in 1525 at the age of 65. His son, John Wynn ap Maredudd – who adopted the surname 'Wynn' – welcomed Leland to Gwydir which then included the Hall of Maredudd and the three-storeyed stair-tower which still survive. John Wynn added the gatehouse (with his initials I.W. 1555) and the rest of the building surrounding a square courtyard. His work was helped by the supply of ready-made materials – dressed stone, windows and choice timber. The abbey at Maenan, only five miles down the Afon Conwy, was dissolved in 1536 and provided the bulk of these materials including one of the finest monastic doors surviving in Wales and now at the head of the spiral stairs. His great grandson, Sir Richard Wynn, built the fine Gwydir Chapel attached to Llanrwst church where he set up a tablet of white marble to the memory of John Wynn ap Maredudd. The inscription (translated from Latin) reads:

Sir John Wynn's House, Gwydir
Medieval stair-tower on the left . . . partly hidden.

Gwydir Castle Gatehouse
J.W. and Coat of Arms

67

John Wynn ap Maredudd, an inheritor of his father's virtues, a just and pious man, to whom Rune, his wife, brought five sons and two daughters. He died on 9th of July 1559.

In visiting Gwydir, Leland was recognising, royal indebtedness to the Wynn family on behalf of Henry VIII. Their extensive knowledge of Snowdonia also may have been helpful to Leland in compiling his extensive list of lakes in the mountains.

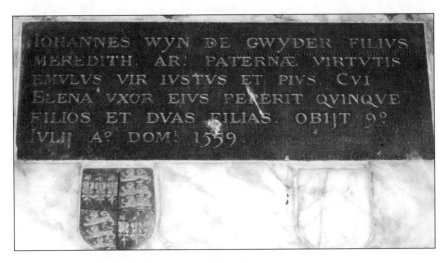

*Memorial tablet to John Wynn of Gwydir
(d. 1559) in Gwydir chapel (Llanrwst Church).*

MEDIEVAL LAKE DISTRICT

Lakes in Snowdonia

A remarkable feature of Leland's itinerary is the amount of local detail which he records about the lakes of Snowdonia. He did not venture into Snowdonia but was aware of the mountains from the time when he saw them from the limestone headlands above Penrhyn Old Hall and later when he crossed the Conwy estuary from Deganwy. Here the Ordovician volcanic rocks of Snowdonia reached the coast at Penmaenmawr. He refers to 'Eryri' ('the high mountains') as Snowdonia and refers to Snowdon itself as *'Withaw'* which is his version of the Welsh name 'Yr Wyddfa'. His interests in Snowdonia were mainly concerned with the large number of lakes about which he gives so much detail that he must have been given this information by the people he met and who knew the area intimately. The lakes are recorded in a precise geographical distribution with facts about their length, breadth, locations and sometimes with a unique feature. The first group mentioned includes Llyn Cwellyn and Llyn y Gadair which lie south of Caernarfon. Cwellyn lies in a valley, is one mile long and noted for its red-bellied char or trout known in Welsh as 'tor-goch'. An interesting description of its neighbour, Llyn y Gadair, which is *'a quarter of a mile in every way'* indicates its almost circular plan. Also in the same area Leland mentions Llyn y Dywarchen as having a *'swimming island'* of earth and turf which floats across the lake during high winds. Here he was using the information given by Gerald of Wales in 1188 who described this floating island which gave its name to the lake. 'Tyarchen' describes a piece of earth – an island or a mound – which is covered with pasture.

The next group mentioned is Llyn Padarn – two miles long – and Llyn Peris which is *'merely a bow-shot from Padarn'* and both provide water for the Afon Seiont which reaches the sea at Caernarfon. Even the small Llyn Dwythwch on the slopes of Snowdon above Nant Peris is named.

To the south of Snowdon he mentions Llyn Dinas (one mile long) and a mile away Llyn Gwynant which both lie in the bottom of the Gwynant Valley. High above these valley lakes on the east side of Snowdon itself he refers to Llyn Llydaw (one mile long) and Llyn Glaslyn which he records with great accuracy as being *'in Withaw (Snowdon) in the highest part and east of Eryri and near Llyn Llydaw'*.

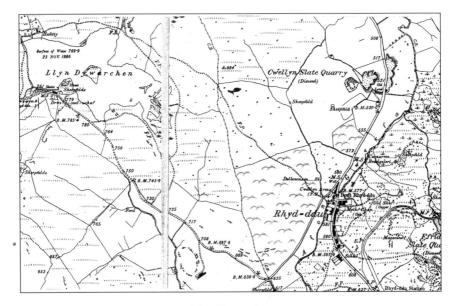

Llyn Dywarchen
The lake with the floating island referred to here by Gerald of Wales who completed
his Itinerary of Wales in 1188. Still shown on O.S. map
'On the highest parts of these mountains are two lakes worthy of admiration. The
one has a floating island in it, which is often driven from one side to the other by
the force of the winds; and the shepherds behold with astonishment their cattle,
whilst feeding, carried to the distant parts of the lake. A part of the bank naturally
bound together by the roots of willows and other shrubs may have been broken off,
and increased by the alluvium of the earth from the shore; and being continually
agitated by the winds, which in so elevated a situation blow with great violence, it
cannot reunite itself firmly with the banks.'

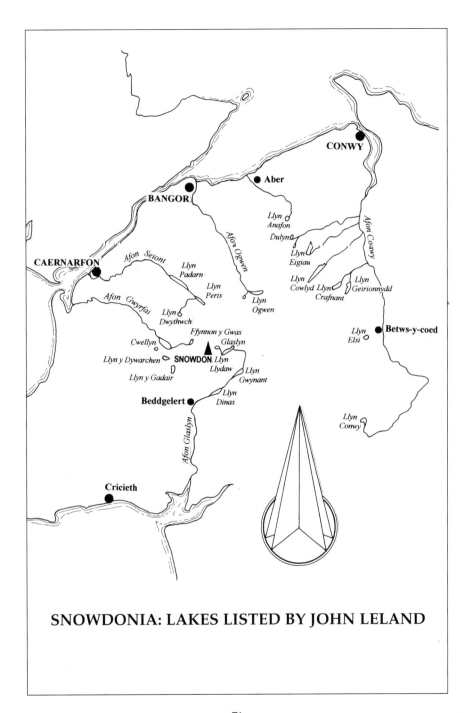

SNOWDONIA: LAKES LISTED BY JOHN LELAND

This accurate description is a credit to his sources since they are the highest and most remote lakes in Snowdonia. There is no possibility that Leland visited such a remote spot; it was not until the end of the next century that botanists penetrated these high summits. However from Leland's account the lakes were well known to the people living in the small hamlets below – Beddgelert, Nant Peris and Capel Curig – and also by the Cistercian monks at Maenan in the Conwy Valley. The monks had access to their monastic granges in Snowdonia and used the high summer pastures (hafotai) for sheep grazing. Even the small lake – Ffynnon y Gwas – just below the high crags of Snowdon is mentioned by Leland.

In a separate group he places Llyn Ogwen (one mile long) five miles south of Bangor which feeds Afon Ogwen which reaches the sea near Penrhyn where Leland probably stayed with Sir Gwilym Gruffydd. Also in the area was Llyn Anafon *'a little pool'* and Llyn Idwal *'a small pool in the Nant Ffrancon valley'*.

In Eastern Snowdonia and flowing into the Afon Conwy he records the main lakes and may have obtained information about them from John Wynn ap Maredudd at Gwydir and probably from the monks at Maenan who would know the area in detail. He comments on two lakes in Caerhun parish – Llyn Dulyn ('the Black Pool') which was less than half a mile long and full of stones; also recorded is Llyn Eigiau which is almost a mile long. Llyn Cowlyd was only one mile south of Eigiau and also in this area was Llyn Crafnant (two miles long) and situated *'two miles south of Conwy Abbey'*.

This lake and its neighbour, Llyn Geirionydd, were both in Llanrhychwyn parish. Other lakes in the area included Ffynnon Llugwy and, above Betws-y-coed, Llyn Elsi.

The recording of the names of the lakes and the details given is remarkable and shows even in the medieval period the extent of the geographical knowledge held by the local people about an area of high mountainous terrain. It also shows the intellectual curiosity of Leland and his ability to organise the geographical data in a manner well ahead of his time.

A COMFORTABLE DAY'S RIDE TO CAERNARFON

Penrhyn and Cochwillan

From Penrhyn Old Hall Leland left the limestone coast of Creuddyn and crossed the Conwy estuary – by ferry – and then followed the difficult cliff-bound path along the seaward edge of Penmaenbach. He then observed the Afon Dwygyfylchi flowing *'by itself into the Menai Salt arm'*.

After passing the steep cliffs of Penmaenmawr the next river he crossed was Afon Llanfairfechan which *'rises in the mountains nearby'*.

The next valley to the west was that of Afon Aber which rises in Llyn Anafon and reaches the sea at Aber. Here there was a church and a motte and bailey castle which was a striking artificial hill called 'Mud' (Mwd). Llywelyn the Great had a castle or palace near the church which was still partly standing according to Leland. The next river was Afon Ogwen which was the biggest river crossed in this section of his journey and had its source in Llyn Ogwen, east of Snowdon.

After this arduous 12-mile journey from Conwy along the well-trodden 'military' road from Conwy Castle to Caernarfon Leland would have been relieved to see the hill-top house overlooking the mouth of the Ogwen – Penrhyn. This magnificent site was occupied by a hall-house belonging (in 1536-9) to Sir Gwilym Gruffydd *'Sir Gul Gruffydd has a fair house at Penrhyn, a mile this side of Bangor'* and had been recorded as early as 1413 as *'placea (plas) penrine'*.

The estate belonged to descendants of Ednyfed Fychan, Seneschal to Llywelyn the Great and they had continued his function as administrators. The builder of the original house was Goronwy ap Tudur whose grandson – Maredudd – was father of Owain Tudur who married Katherine de Valois, widow of Henry V, and later created the Tudor dynasty. His daughter married into a local family – Gruffydd – and on Leland's visit the house belonged to Sir Gwilym Gruffydd, who was the main government official in northern Wales. He had only a few years earlier rebuilt and extended the house at Penrhyn. This eventually in 1827 was replaced by Penrhyn Castle which incorporated the old house but some of the old 15th century features were re-used. Fragments of 15th century window lights similar to those in Caernarfon Castle were

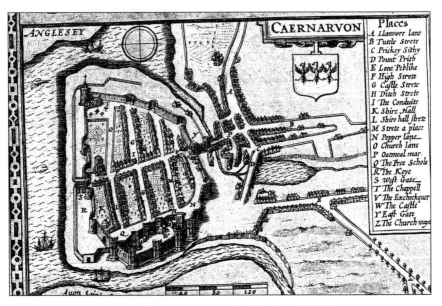

Caernarfon – town plan – by John Speed (1610)
Note – West Gate and East Gate and bridge over Cadnant River
D – shows the 'Pount Prith' or Bont Bridd, earth dam over the Afon Cadnant.

Penrhyn Castle
The medieval chapel rebuilt outside
the 19th century castle.

retained in the hall; an arched doorway and stone stair-turret were found recently under dislodged masonry. The medieval chapel which was in the old house was removed (in 1827) stone by stone into the park and is a feature of the present landscape. A chapel inside a house was a mark of wealth and status. Leland would have been impressed by the view of Snowdonia from the grounds of Penrhyn and perhaps was given the names and information about the rivers and lakes which were of great interest to him.

Before reaching Penrhyn Leland had visited Cochwillan only two and a half miles to the south where: 'William *ap William lives at a plas – Cochwillan – a mile this side of Penrhyn.'*

This house was also in the Gruffydd family – the younger (cadet) branch – and probably built between 1450 and 1480 by his father, William ap Gruffydd. He had led a troop of horse in support of Henry Tudor at the Battle of Bosworth (1485) and afterwards was made, uniquely, High Sheriff of Caernarfonshire for life.

It was built as a hall-house with a large hall with a wooden screen dividing it from the kitchen and buttery. The hall was open to the roof and a striking feature were the hammer beams and trusses which were elaborately carved; this was an indication of wealth and status. This fine 15th century house has survived to the present day but by the 1880s it had become a shippon and hayloft. A photograph taken in 1913 shows that the building was substantially intact with the south wall composed of large stones fitted together with great skill. The stone arched doorway led directly into the hall and the windows with carved stone tracery were part of the original house. This building was restored in the 1970s and preserves many of the features of the house which Leland visited.

Leland probably crossed the Afon Ogwen just below Cochwillan where the river was divided by an island and could be forded. He then followed the track to Penrhyn.

Leaving Penrhyn he crossed Afon Cegin which flowed into the Menai Strait (*'shore'*) where there was a creek *'a little coming-in for boats from Menai'* and later became Port Penrhyn which exported slates from the quarries at Bethesda. He then passed through the small settlement at Bangor which had two annual fairs and a market. There were a few rows of terraced cottages around the market cross but its chief feature was the Cathedral which he probably visited. He then followed the track towards Caernarfon crossing Afon Pwll where there was *'a little creek for boats to go to Anglesey'* which is now Port Dinorwig (Y Felinheli) which later, in the 19th and 20th centuries, also became an important slate-exporting port. Leland showed a remarkable appreciation of these sites and perhaps an anticipation of their future importance. On the opposite side a small headland jutting into the Menai Strait called Moel-y-don was the *'place for ferry boats to go into Anglesey'*.

A few miles further on Leland noted a brook called Gwenwynmeirch (Horses' Poison) which flowed from a well and entered the Menai east of Caernarfon.

Leland was now approaching Caernarfon which was a large, walled town around the castle but had outgrown its medieval walls. It was an important harbour for ships coming in from the Menai *'hard against the side of the castle.'*

Caernarfon was at the mouth of Afon Seiont but another river Afon Cadnant flows under the town bridge and flows independently into the *'Menai Arm'*. Speed's map of Caernarfon (1610) again confirms this description by Leland who probably stayed in the castle, probably with John Puleston the Constable of the Castle, whom he mentions by name *'Puleston in Caernarfon town'*.

Cochwillan
Courtesy: private owners of the hall

Cochwillan: a 15th century hall-house (fireplace added later).

Cochwillan
Courtesy: private owners of the hall

It was the end of a comfortable day's ride, well within the comfort margin of under ten miles most of which was relatively flat after leaving Bangor and with beautiful views of the Menai Strait and Anglesey.

At the time of Leland's visit Caernarfon was a large medieval walled town at the northern end of the Castle in a 'peninsula' between the Afon Seiont and the marshy estuary of Afon Cadnant. It was chosen in 1284 by Edward I as the site of a large castle and borough with two gates – the West Gate overlooking the Menai Strait and the East Gate (and bridge) to the 'mainland' across Afon Cadnant. It was chosen as the administrative centre of Caernarfonshire. Leland probably stayed in Caernarfon with John Puleston who was the Constable of the Castle. Strangely Leland only mentions Caernarfon briefly with little reference to the size or layout of the town. He does not even mention the massive engineering project completed in the summer of 1285 of the earth dam (PONT BRIDD) across Afon Cadnant. The dam created a large pool ("The King's Pool") which provided fish and water for the town mill. John Speed's superb town plan (1610) shows the features of the town almost exactly as Leland would have seen them on his way through the narrow streets to the castle. The map shows 'POUNT PRITH' (BONT PRIDD) and the expansion of the town eastwards beyond the town walls. Today the only trace of this pool is Pool Street.

A THREAT TO THE 'THREE SHIRES'

'South Croke'

Leland's journey through Wales took place during the summers of 1536-9. The King had gained great wealth from the 'dissolution' of the monasteries; their goods, lands and property were sold off or leased. By 1537 the King's authority was solidly based and he had carried out the breach with the Roman Catholic church with little internal dissension. His main plan in 1537 was to build the greatest palace in Europe – even outrivaling the chateau at Chambord – at Nonsuch only six miles south-east of Hampton Court where he destroyed a village and the church. However in Europe the situation was bleak; the Emperor Charles and Francis, the King of France, were now in alliance and were keen on supporting the Pope's aim to restore Catholicism in England. In response to this threat Henry put money into building up the navy and ordered the building of specially-designed artillery forts especially in Cornwall. He built two 'castles' at St Mawes and Pendennis to guard the entrance to Carrick Roads near Falmouth. The Kent coast around Dover was also fortified as a precaution against a long-threatened Catholic attack from the continent. The population in these areas were mustered, drilled and prepared beacons to signal an attack. Stone from the monasteries was hauled to the coastal areas to build defences and even Henry VIII made "painful journeys" to the coasts to inspect ships and their heavy cannon.

This was the background against which Leland visited Wales apart from his interest in the coastal geography – capes, bays, creeks – and rivers and his intention to make a map. Even northern Wales, especially the Llŷn peninsula, Menai Strait and Anglesey, were also thought to be a target for attack or invasion.. In 1539 Sir Richard Bulkeley, the Chamberlain of northern Wales, received an instruction from Henry VIII to survey the coast and give advice as to its defence. Sir Richard replied to Thomas Cromwell, Henry's Chancellor, with a list of *the names of all the havens, bays, creeks and roads (anchorages) in the three shires'*. These were the original Edward I's counties – Anglesey, Caernarfon and Meirionnydd. Bulkeley was concerned with the western entrance to the Menai Strait at Abermenai. This was a line of sand and low sand-dunes extending from Anglesey across the western end of the Menai Strait. Its extremity curved back on itself – and almost closed the entrance; the opposite side had been

Western Caernarfonshire
John Speed's map – 1610

named *'South Croke'* in the time of Edward I and mentioned by Leland *'South Croke is three miles above Caernarfon and is the very point (end) of Abermenai'*.

In his letter to Cromwell Sir Richard Bulkeley stated that a fortress should be made at South Croke to protect Caernarfon and the entrance to the Menai Strait.

MEDIEVAL CHURCH-BUILDING BOOM IN LLŶN (1500-1535)

Leland's Journey through Llŷn

The next stage of Leland's itinerary took him from Caernarfon westwards to Aberdaron and then along the south coast eastwards to Penrhyndeudraeth. He left Caernarfon castle and then crossed a succession of rivers – the Afon Gwyrfai, which he crossed at Bontnewydd (New Bridge), then a series of brooks flowing into y Foryd – a tidal arm at the western entrance to the Menai Strait. The next river crossed was the Afon Llyfni at Pontllyfni and then the short Afon Desach *'going by itself to the sea'*.

The track was flat and straight and always within sight of the sea; it led directly to Clynnog-fawr which was, at this stage, his main objective and the start of the 'Pilgrim's Trail' to Bardsey Island (*Ynys Enlli*). This was a well-worn path dating from the Middle Ages when three visits to Bardsey – the 'island of a thousand saints' – was equivalent to one visit to Rome. Along this route churches were dotted at regular intervals and even roadside stone crosses marked its course. In the 7th century A.D. the Celtic Saints – notably St Beuno in this area – had built their small wooden churches ('Llannau'). St Beuno was the most venerated saint here and his reputed burial-place (on 21st April 642) was at Clynnog-fawr. Ten churches on either side of Caernarfon Bay are dedicated to St Beuno. Some of the masonry under St Beuno's chapel at Clynnog was found in 1913 and dated to the original 7th century monastery. An inscribed stone to Beuno – Maen Beuno – with a simple Christian cross is preserved in the church and a short distance away in St Beuno's well which was a holy well attracting pilgrims to the shrine.

According to Leland Clynnog-fawr was 'the fairest church in Caernarfonshire and better than Bangor'.

By 1291 it had become a collegiate church with four canons who lived there, and was receiving endowments from estates in Anglesey and Caernarfonshire as far east as Bangor. Its prosperity was also due to revenue from pilgrims and with the popularity of pilgrimages after the Wars of the Roses this money was used for extensions to the church. About 1500 the nave was added to the chancel and just before Leland's

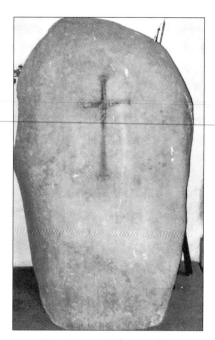

Clynnog-fawr Church
Two-storey living accommodation above
entrance porch.Staircase (modern)
to medieval door.

Maen Beuno – Clynnog-fawr
7th – 9th century stone found at
Bontnewydd. Probably a prayer-stone
on Pilgrims' trail. Stop for prayer
before moving on.

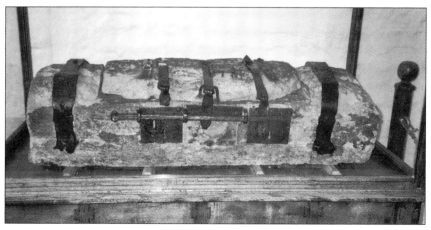

Cyff Beuno, Clynnog-fawr.
Medieval oak chest . . . later (1608) padlocked. Held parish records and charity offerings.

visit the tall western tower was built and the north porch with living accommodation for the canons on two floors was added and as a separate building St Beuno's Chapel was built over the medieval chapel and shrine of St Beuno. The architecture of the church was therefore transformed (1500-1535) only a year or so before Leland visited Clynnog. He was an eye-witness to these changes *'the church which is now there with cross-aisles is almost as big as St David's but it is of new work'* and *'the old church where St Beuno is buried hard by the new'*.

Although it was a collegiate church and had been a monastery, it was not destroyed by the Act of Dissolution of the Monasteries and survived as a parish church. It continued to prosper and the local family – the Glynnes – with the family eagle at the entrance to the stalls and the misericords are the finest in Caernarfonshire and also date to this period. It is probable that with living accommodation available Leland stayed at Clynnog which was only ten miles from Caernarfon – an ideal day's ride. It has remained largely unaltered since Leland's visit except for the addition of a narrow dark passage (17th century) linking Beuno's chapel with the Tower.

Leaving Clynnog the track ran past Llanaelhaearn church with its holy well and the pilgrim stone cross built into the church wall over the pass south of Yr Eifl (Mountains). The next 'station' was Pistyll where *'there comes out of a rock a small rill or brook as if it was running in a pipe'*.

This comment based on his observation is a good description of the word 'pistyll' – a spout. The church was a plain single-chamber with some 12th century walls and conical font still intact. The field above on Cefnydd hill was called 'Cae hospice' used to accommodate overnight stops for pilgrims. Leland continued on to the small 'townlet' of Nefyn which had two fairs a year but no weekly market.

Leland had little time to visit all the churches but must have been aware of the fine church at Llangwnnadl with its three aisles which was also undergoing massive rebuilding about 1520-30. With its shrine to the saint and the field adjacent to the church called Cae Eisteddfa (sitting field) it was a major stop for pilgrims. Eventually he reached Aberdaron which he describes as a 'small townlet of Aberdaron where there are 30 or more houses on the further side of the Afon Daron and the sea is about a quarter of a mile away'.

For some reason the notes at this point are missing and it is unlikely that Leland would not have mentioned the church of St Hywyn which

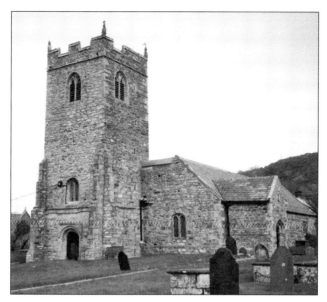

Llanengan Church (tower and porch)
facing Bardsey Island. Built just before Leland's visit.

Latin inscription – blocks of gritstone with date 1534
above west door of the tower at Llanengan Church.

was on the edge of a sandy beach. The church at Aberdaron was also extended in the early 16th century when a south nave was built alongside the north nave (with its fine 12th century doorway) separated by an arcade of five arches. This was the final church where pilgrims waited for suitable weather and tidal conditions to make the crossing to Bardsey. They walked along the cliff path to the cove at Porth Meudwy and then took a boat along the coast to Pen y Cil and thence across the treacherous Bardsey Sound to the southern tip of the island. They would then walk the length of the island to St Mary's Abbey. When the abbey was dissolved in 1536-7 it lost it lands, property and status as a place for pilgrimage.

Leland then turned eastwards from Aberdaron and keeping to the coast for about eight miles with superb views over the sandy bay of Porth Neigwl (Hell's Mouth) reached Llanengan. Here, about a mile from the sea he visited and stopped at the parish church *'where recently there was a great pilgrimage'*.

He must have been impressed by the numbers visiting the shrine to St Einion and the holy well nearby. Money donated by the pilgrims placed in the ancient wooden chest (Cyff Engan) was used in the rebuilding boom of the 1520-1530 period. The arcade similar to that at Llangwnnadl (with an inscribed stone dated 1520) and the high West Tower had transformed its appearance. It gave spectacular views across Porth Neigwl with an uninterrupted view of Bardsey Island and was the only mainland church with a view of the island. A room had been built for the custodian over the south porch – similar to the one built at Clynnog – and a garderobe for him reached from the Tower in 1534 and only two years before Leland's visit. The Tower can be dated with certainty because above the west door there is a Latin inscription:

THIS BELFRY WAS BUILT IN HONOUR OF ST EINION, KING OF WALES, APOSTLE OF THE SCOTS, A.D. 1534

It consists of 26 small blocks of gritstone with Tudor badges of the pomegranate, fleur-de-lys and rose; the inscription has been badly weathered on the stormy west-facing side of the church.

It is highly probable that Leland stayed at Llanengan because of its status as a wealthy church and there were comfortable lodging facilities.

He continued eastwards to the cliffs of Penrhyn Du – now overlooking

Abersoch – with views of the two St Tudwal's Islands and the deserted church on the main island. From there he passed through Pwllheli which had a *'poor market'* and Cricieth which was once a borough but now had only *'two or three poor houses'* and was in decay below its cliff-top castle. From Cricieth he followed the coast to the wide sandy estuary of Traeth Mawr which he crossed (probably at Minffordd) to the high wooded peninsula of Penrhyndeudraeth which separated it from Traeth Bach. There were *'salt arms and creeks fed with no notable fresh rivers'*.

It was here that he mentioned Mr Rowland Griffith from Anglesey who gave him much information about the coastlands to the south which they could see from Penrhyndeudraeth.

Llanengan Church
Inscription in Latin above the west door of Belfrey – dated 1534.
Built in honour of St Einion.

'HOUSES AND HOSPITALITY IN LLŶN'

From Llanengan eastwards along the south coast of Llŷn, Leland does not mention any churches but there were a number of houses which he recorded with the names of their owners who probably provided a safe haven and hospitality. He seems to have been following a course about one or two miles from the coast and after leaving Pwllheli – 'a poor town' – he would inevitably have passed Pennarth Fawr. This was a fine hall-house recorded in the mid 15th century as belonging to Madog ap Hywel and by Leland's time was in the hands of his grandson William ap Howell who died in 1540. His son adopted the surname 'Wynn' as part of the policy of replacing 'ap' (son of) in favour of a surname which would be easier to record in the now-compulsory parish registers (1536). The hall-house was built of massive uncoursed boulders in the foundations and was the standard 'cyclopean' style found in north-west Wales where loose stone was abundant. The remarkable features were the finely-carved roof timbers and the aisle trusses which were more typical of the wooded valleys of north-east Wales. These trusses were thick oak timbers rising vertically to the roof on each side of the open hall leaving spaces or aisles between them and the walls. Partitions and screens separating the hall from the kitchen and an open-hearth fire would have given comfort and some privacy. The house has been restored to its original plan and apart from the large fireplace built and date-inscribed in 1615 Leland would have no difficulty in recognising the house. Another house on his way towards Criccieth was Rhosgyll Fawr which was also a 15th century hall-house of large boulders in the foundations, the corners and even the sides where they project from the walls. At the time of Leland's journey the owner was Humphrey Lloyd ap Dafydd who had married Jane, daughter of William Glynne, Serjeant at Arms to Henry VIII. When the house was restored in 1975 a child's leather shoe was found hidden in the wall of the chimney breast and was confirmed by Cardiff University as a medieval shoe placed deliberately in the original house. In 1528 Rhosgyll Fawr and its pastures were transferred to nearby Talhenbont as the local gentry were consolidating their estates.

On this section of his journey Leland mentions four houses and perhaps felt obliged to name their owners for their help and support:

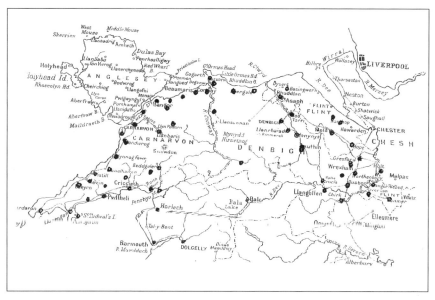

Place named in Leland's Litherary

Rhosgyll Fawr – 15th century house built of local boulders collected from the fields. 'Cyclopean' style of architecture.

Medieval leather shoe (child's) found in the chimney of Rhosgyll Fawr near Cricieth.

Pennarth Fawr
Front of the house shows late 15th century building – arched doorway and roughly-coursed local boulders. Window frames, roof and chimney are 18th century and later.

Pennarth Fawr
Medieval hall-house showing finely-carved roof timbers – decorative style shows wealth and status of late 15th century owner.

John ap Madog	-	at Bodfel
Griffith ap Robert	-	at Talhenbont
John Owen	-	in an *'ancient house at Kegid'*
Elys ap Morris	-	in Llanmorfa parish at Clennennau

All of these houses still exist but not as Leland would have known them. Bodfel and Talhenbont were both rebuilt in 1607; only the cellar at Talhenbont survives from the Hen Blas (Old Plas). *'Kegid'* refers to Ystymcegid and this was also rebuilt after Leland's time but outbuildings survive which retain features belonging to the old house. One barn at Ystumcegid retains re-used 16th century joists and grooved mouldings and another one has the roof trusses of the same period. All the houses were built of stone and slate and were typical of Snowdonia. The owners were men of wealth and status who belonged to families who had helped to found the Tudor dynasty. Before Leland's visit *'Kegid'* was the home of John ap Maredudd who helped in Henry VII's victory at Bosworth. His son, John Owen, lived in the *'ancient house'*. John ap Maredudd's eldest son had been given land nearby to build Plas Clennennau which was inherited by Elys who was only in his twenties when Leland visited. Here a barn which is mortised for post and panel partition of late 15th century date is part of the original house.

Plotting the locations of these houses gives a clue to Leland's route to what may have been his final stop in Llŷn. He finally reached the promontory at Penrhyndeudraeth with marvellous views of the sandy estuary of Traeth Mawr and Traeth Bach.

'MR ROWLAND GRIFFITH FROM ANGLESEY TOLD ME . . . '

A Valuable Source of Information

An interesting episode in the history of Clynnog-fawr church occurred in 1536 at the time of the Dissolution of the Monasteries. Clynnog was a 'royal foundation' having been acquired by the King following the Conquest of Wales and the transfer of the rights of the Welsh princes who had donated lands to the church at Clynnog. During the Middle Ages, Clynnog had become a collegiate church with four canons living there and extensive lands in Caernarfonshire and Anglesey. Just before Leland's visit the little chapel of St Beuno had been rebuilt and united with a much larger structure with a fine West Tower. With the impending threat from the Dissolution of the Monasteries a High Court case was held in Caernarfon between Henry VIII and the Bishop of Bangor concerning the right of patronage in the church and the disposal of church property. However it was decided that Clynnog did not come within the scope of the Act because it was not wealthy enough with only an income of less than £200 per annum and it was not a monastery. It was 'visited' in 1536, its property confiscated, and it became an ordinary parish church. The King was determined to reduce the chances of the 'spoil' falling into the hands of the local squires. The commissioners met in November 1537 and one of the principal witnesses was Rowland Griffith 'of the county of Anglesey' who confirmed that the church was under the authority of the "chief lord" (Henry VIII) from an earlier manuscript deposition. He added that the King was patron of Clynnog with Llangeinwen and Llangaffo (in Anglesey). He was a very important witness and as such would have met Leland – probably at Clynnog – and perhaps accompanied him on his journey through Llŷn.

This may explain how, when he reached Penrhyndeudraeth, Leland made a reference to Rowland Griffith who gave him valuable information:

> 'Mr Rowland Griffith told me that there were two commotes between Aberdyfi and Tywyn and in times past the area was rich in corn and grass but being low-lying and level the sea, many years ago, had flooded it and it was now a sandy wilderness.'

Llanddwyn Island looking west towards Yr Eifl, Llŷn.
Now a peninsula with sand bar linking it to the mainland.

Trwyn y Penrhyn
View of the Afon Glaslyn Traeth Mawr (sand) and
Penrhyndeudraeth Peninsula from Borth-y-gest.

Leland said that Rowland Griffith told him that the church where he lived in Anglesey was in ancient times a house of religion. He continued to give Leland information about the area south of Penrhyndeudraeth. Leland refers to Harlech castle and market town and, further south, Cymer Abbey. Dolgellau was the *'best village in the commote'* and further south Machynlleth had a bridge over the Afon Dyfi. It is unlikely that Leland continued southwards and relied heavily on basic information acquired at second-hand from his friend, Rowland Griffith.

Although Leland compiled a record of the main parish churches and their dependent chapels in Anglesey there is no evidence that he crossed the Menai Strait to visit the island. He gives a list complied by a Welsh copyist and records the geographical features – islands, lakes, bays and settlements such as Beaumaris and Newborough. He was using official papers which named the churches and the rents they received – in all thirty-one churches, or *llannau*, were named. Only a year or so before – in 1535 – the value of ecclesiastical properties called the 'Valor Ecclesiasticus' was compiled. The parish priest and four reliable persons had to declare the true value of the benefice. Leland had to rely on second-hand information such as that given to him by Mr Rowland Griffith about the submerged forests, the 'new' stone walls around the fields and the earthenware pots with human bone and ash. However in one special reference he gives a detailed account of Llanddwyn island which lies off the south-west corner of Anglesey:

'Ther is in Mone as right againe Neuen tounne in Lline, there a kenning of, a little isle caullid Sainct Dunwen, a woman, and in this isle is the chirch of S. Dunwen. This isle is veri fertile of cunnies, and hath ii fair welles. Ther is now a little balk of sand cast up, the wich at low waters prohibitith the se to cum about.'

['There is in Anglesey, opposite the town of Nefyn in Llŷn, a good view of the small island of Saint Dwynwen, a woman, and the island has a church of Saint Dwynwen. The island is overrun by rabbits and has two good wells. There is now a small ridge of sand which has been cast up and at low water prevents the sea from separating the island from the mainland.']

This passage was probably inspired by Leland's view of the island as he made his way along the Pilgrim Trail from Clynnog to Nefyn. The peninsula of Llanddwyn was a place of pilgrimage and a prominent landmark visible from the shore between Clynnog-fawr and further south as far as Nefyn. Although Leland mentions Nefyn it is probable that he saw the island from Clynnog where he stayed overnight – the range of sight over a distance of only eight miles across the bay is totally unobstructed.

The church of St Dwynwen had a chancel and transepts similar in proportion to those of Clynnog and the windows were similar in appearance to late 15th century work at Bangor Cathedral. Although now in ruins the high walls remain and the window frames with their dressed stone indicate its importance. The two wells have survived – Ffynnon Dafaden (Sheep's Well) which resembles a square sheep-fold and Saint Dwynwen's well near the shore.

The island can still be reached across the sand bar and high sand-dunes cover the rock outcrops. There is a strong possibility that the mysterious Mr Rowland Griffith met Leland at Clynnog and gave him the information about Llanddwyn island which they could see across the bay.

The church was one of the chief benefices in the Diocese of Bangor with offerings from the many visitors who came to see the sacred relics and visit the holy wells. Leland probably knew that just over fifty years earlier an incumbent at Llanddwyn, Richard Kyffin, had secretly corresponded with Henry VIII's father – Henry VII – then the Earl of Richmond who was in exile in Brittany, and his main supporter, Rhys ap Thomas, in Pembroke. Letters of support were sent by boat to Rhys ap Thomas urging Richmond to return and overthrow Richard III. The knowledge of this support from Llanddwyn probably accounts for Leland's interest in the island and his reference to it would have gained the approval of his patron, Henry VIII.

At the time of Leland's visit Sir Gwilym Gruf, Chamberlain of northern Wales, lived in the 'fair house' of Plas Penrhyn, near Bangor. Earlier the Griffith family had purchased land and a house – Llwyn-y-Moel – on the Anglesey side of the Menai Strait. The house had been rebuilt by Robert Griffith about 1500 and, by Leland's time, had passed to his eldest son, Rowland. The area was rich in pasture, meadow and patches of woodland ('llwyn'). Its fertility was marked by the numerous *plasdai* – Plas Coch, Plas Cefn Mawr, Plas Porthamel, Plas Llwynnon and Plas Llanedwen. It also included the isolated parish church of Llanedwen and the valuable ferry-crossing to Caernarfon at Moel-y-don. Rowland

Griffith's first marriage was to Catherine, daughter of Maredudd ap Ieuan of Gwydir in the Conwy Valley. His second marriage was to Agnes, daughter of Morris ap Maredudd of Clenennau who was another substantial landowner. With these family connections Rowland Griffith would have been well-informed about church affairs, politics and the geography of Caernarfonshire and Anglesey. He was also interested in archaeology, history, rural customs and farming. He was principal witness in the court case of 1537 at Caernarfon in support of Henry VIII's claim to be patron of Clynnog-fawr church. Leland acknowledges the information given by Rowland Griffith who may have facilitated his journey through Llŷn and Caernarfonshire and may have acted as a guide. The detailed notes on Clynnog-fawr church and Llanddwyn island show the 'hand' of Rowland Griffith.

Llanddwyn Island
Ruins of St Dwynwen's church – east window of the chancel
and side window overlooking the Menai Strait.

96

PUTTING WALES ON THE MAP

Humphrey Llwyd's Map of Wales (1573)

Humphrey Llwyd (1527-1568) aged 34, 1561, wearing black doublet, gold chain, prayer book, Coat of Arms, Motto – 'Hwy pery klod na golyd' (Fame lasts longer than wealth).

When Leland set off on his journey around Wales in 1536 he had no maps to help him plan his route. He had a list of places to visit – churches, monasteries, cathedrals, castles and towns. He also had a list of prominent men who could provide hospitality and guides who could give him local information. His eventual intention was to produce a map showing the courses of rivers, lakes and places of interest with distances and directions. Wales in 1536 was not depicted on a map which could be of any practical use. The only 'maps' showed Wales as a spherical or square area of land separated from England by the River Dee and River Severn. Two years before he set out an anonymous map showed Wales as a square-shaped mass with some rivers such as the Dee, Conwy, Severn and with a large island, Anglesey, in the north-west.

It was not until after Henry VIII's reign that maps appeared giving Wales a recognisable shape. By the early years of Elizabeth's reign there were three maps – by Lawrence Nowell, Gerard Mercator and Humphrey Llwyd (or Lhuyd) – which gave Wales an outline which could be of use to the explorer. For the first time the great peninsulas of Llŷn and

Pembrokeshire as well as the Dee estuary and Milford Haven are shown.

At this time Gerard Mercator was the leading cartographer and was involved in the new techniques of mapping using triangulation surveys, which provided accurate distances, as well as printing styles and engraving on copper plates. The centre of map making was Flanders and particularly the mercantile city of Antwerp. Trade between Antwerp and London was conducted through the Royal Exchange which was in the control of Sir Thomas Gresham. His chief factor in Antwerp was 'Sir' Richard Gough who came from Denbigh and knew Humphrey Llwyd's family who had property at Henllan just outside the town. This 'network' explains how Llwyd became involved in the focus of map making then flourishing in Antwerp.

Humphrey Llwyd was born at Foxhall (originally Faulkes Hall named after his grandfather) – an important hall-house one mile north of Denbigh – in 1527, whose ancestors had come in with the Earl of Lincoln in 1297 to oversee the Lordship of Denbigh after the Conquest. He was educated at Brasenose College, Oxford and then entered the service of Henry Fitzalan, Earl of Arundel. When Elizabeth came to the throne (in 1558) Fitzalan became the powerful Lord Steward of the Queen's Household. He was so important to Elizabeth that she granted him the lease of Nonsuch Palace near London built by Henry VIII to outshine all palaces in Europe including Chambord in France. Llwyd gained valuable experience and contacts in the Royal Court and travelled with Fitzalan in Europe as far as Italy and returning through Flanders. His main academic interests were in History and Antiquarian subjects and he gained access to valuable manuscripts – including Leland's in the Fitzalan and Royal Libraries. A contemporary portrait by an unknown artist (in 1561) shows the 34-year old Humphrey Llwyd with a fashionable square beard, white ruff collar, three gold chains, a black gown and, in a gloved hand, a book to denote learning and scholarship. He remained a member of the Fitzalan household for the rest of his life and became an MP for East Grinstead in Elizabeth's first Parliament in 1559. He also retained his interest in his native town of Denbigh and lived within the walls of the castle in his later years. He became an Alderman and took and active interest in the affairs of the town. He travelled to Italy in 1566-67 and on his return journey at Antwerp was introduced by his merchant friend, Richard Gough, to Abraham Ortelius. He was at this time collecting information for an Atlas, and was anxious to get as much information

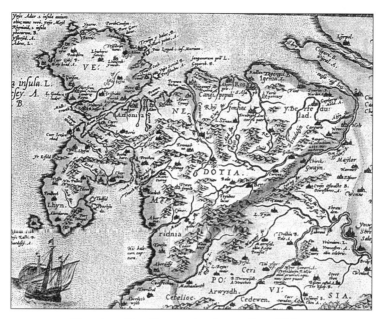

Humphrey Llwyd's map showing northern Wales.

Foxhall, near Henllan home of Humphrey Llwyd.

about Wales as possible and knew about Llwyd's knowledge of Welsh history and places. They agreed to correspond and Llwyd promised to send his notes on Anglesey with facts about rivers, towns and places of note. The letter was sent on 5th April 1568 but Llwyd had contracted a fever after his travels and knowing that he would not recover he sent Ortelius his notes and maps. His map of Wales he acknowledged was 'not beautifully set forth in all its points, yet truly depicted'. It did contain inaccuracies but was a great improvement on earlier maps. He did not live to see his map printed from its fine, copper engraving and was subsequently printed so many times that it became merely an historical document. Christopher Saxton shortly afterwards produced a more detailed map of Wales based on basic surveying methods and in 1610 John Speed produced a map of the counties of Wales including a marvellous town-plan of Denbigh which Llwyd would have greatly appreciated. Speed's map of Denbighshire also included Llwyd's house at Foxhall which he prints as 'Foxhole'.

Humphrey Llwyd can be credited with the first recognisable map of Wales with over three hundred place-names. Apart from the map he collected an impressive library and with that of his benefactor Henry Fitzalan and his son-in-law, the books and manuscripts were bought by James I and formed the basis of the Royal Collection now in the British Library. The plaque near the door of the present house at Foxhall, records:

HUMPHREY LLWYD; ANTIQUARIAN

This claim is fully justified because of his famous book 'CRONICA WALLIA' (1559) which is an English adaptation of the 'BRUT Y TWYSOGION' which records the history of Wales from the 8th century to 1284.

In producing his map of Wales he used existing maps that were available, including Mercator's, and added his own knowledge of places gained by travel and reading. He would have been familiar with John Leland's 'Itinerary' from his original manuscripts. He corrected what he believed were mistakes in Leland's spelling of Welsh words and his confusion over 'V' and 'Y' – 'the ignorance whereof did cause much trouble to my friend, Mr Leland'. The general outline shown on Llwyd's map is good but the end of the Llŷn peninsula is grossly distorted with the end curving southwards into Cardigan Bay. Much of the interior of Wales was unsafe for travellers and yet his map shows rivers which extend far into the remote areas. The Dee is shown with its tributaries – Twrch and Lliw – flowing into Bala Lake. The River Conwy is shown rising in the remote Llyn Conwy. The rivers are correctly spelled and he probably used information from Leland. This attention to detail is evident also in the place-names of towns and villages which are shown by a building symbol. The places are spaced fairly accurately and a contemporary traveller could use the map for his journey. By following the Dee he could travel from Chester and follow its course via Holt, Llangollen, Corwen to Bala. The mountains are clearly marked by shaded symbols which resemble 'molehills' but no attempt was made to indicate scale. In northern Wales only two mountains are named – Snowdon Hill and Cader. The lowland areas are shown clearly as white spaces. Along the coast there is attention to detail as shown by the small islands of Tudwal's (near Abersoch) and Ynys Seiriol which would aid navigation for ships similar to the three-masted vessel in the corner of the map. He introduced cartographic devices introduced earlier by Mercator including the use of pictorial views of buildings to show towns and villages. The mountains are shown in realistic positions and his 'Snowdon Hill' is a direct copy of 'Snowdon Hylle' on the Mercator map. The major features are shown in Roman letterings – VENEDOTIA – for Gwynedd. For most places they are evenly spread into smaller 'italic' print, for example, Bala. The high quality of the engraved lettering was cut by a sharp-pointed burin on copper plate.

Sadly Humphrey Llwyd never lived to see his map published (in 1573) because he died of fever on 21st August 1568. He was buried at Whitchurch, the parish church on the outskirts of Denbigh inside the north aisle. Here an alabaster memorial records the epigraph:

HUMFREY LLOID, MR OF ARTS;
A FAMOUS WORTHY WIGHT [Man]

His portrait of 1561 was probably commissioned by his patron, the Earl of Arundel, and in 1578 an obituary in gold lettering was added to the painting. The coat of arms of his family – including a stag and a lion – was placed in his house at Foxhall and this is the earliest recorded heraldic shield (1568) still surviving in northern Wales. The practice of displaying a coat of arms spread rapidly in the next hundred years and the largest number can be claimed for the houses of the lesser gentry and yeomen in the Vale of Clwyd. The coat of arms at Foxhall is an appropriate tribute to Humphrey Llwyd as an antiquarian scholar with an interest in his family history with the motto:

HWY PER Y GLÔD NA GOLYD
THEY CAUSE PRAISE RATHER THAN HARM

displayed on his portrait.

His fame rests largely on his map of Wales which completed what his friend, John Leland, had intended.

'A MAP WITH WORDS'

Leland was travelling without maps and his intention was to produce a 'map with words' – he continually gives distances and directions. This is well shown when he reached Llangollen and passed from Bromfield into the adjoining Lordship of Yale. Having crossed Bromfield he entered Yale (Iâl) which was *'upon the farther side of the River Dee'* which was the north side and included the castle of Dinas Brân and the abbey at Valle Crucis. South of the River Dee was the Lordship of Chirk.

Having defined the boundaries of Yale Leland was ready to leave Valle Crucis and make his way northwards into the mountains of Yale. The only way was to follow the River Eglwyseg which flowed past the abbey and then follow a steep-sided tributary. His notebooks give sufficient information even without place-names to trace his route because of the telling details about the landscape. From Valle Crucis he followed the valley bottom to what is now the hamlet of Pentredwr. He then followed a steep horse-track along the sides of the narrow tributary ravine to the summit of the pass at over 1300 feet. This is now the site occupied by the Ponderosa Café. He climbed 700 feet in a mile with a precipitous slope on the right-hand side before reaching the moorland. He describes the abrupt change in the landscape by contrasting it with the valley at Valle Crucis with its densely wooded slopes and corn and meadows along the river. On the moorland plateau sheep and goats grazed the short grass and heather which had been the site of the medieval grange of Valle Crucis. It was the site of the abbot's summer house (Hafod yr Abad) and an old church (Hen Eglwys). The area was so high and windswept that there were no trees and the local shepherds used peat as their main fuel.

Leland knew that he was now on the 'other' side of the watershed and defined his position with reference to a castle now known as Tomen-y-Rhodwydd – a striking motte and bailey – built in 1149 by Owain Gwynedd to strengthen his position against Powys (in the Dee Valley). Leland comments that:

> *'almost in the middle point between Valle Crucis and Ruthin there appears the vestiges of a castle of Owain Glyndŵr (as it is said) called Cefn Du . . . where shepherds now keep sheep.'*

It is probable that Leland, being unfamiliar with Welsh history, may have

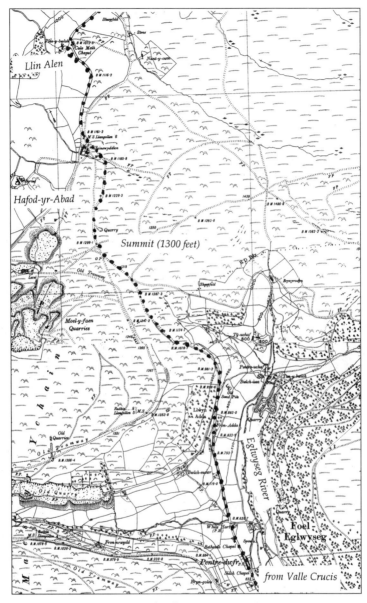

Leland's route . . .
Route taken by Leland from Valle Crucis – through Pentredŵr, then up track
to summit at over 1300 feet. Over the watershed with Hafod yr Abad on the left
and the source of the River Alun –'Llyn Alun'.

been misinformed about its date and builder by his local guide. The castle is still there and the farmer still keeps sheep!

Leland records the location of 'Lin Alen' which was the source of the River Alun *'The greatest water beside the Dee in the whole of Yale'*.

'Llin Alen' (Llyn Alun) was a misnomer because it was merely a small pool but even today never runs dry and is fed by abundant rainfall, high-level springs and saturated moss and peat. It is not shown on modern maps but its exact location is known by the local farmers and is the source of the river. It lies just below the track which Leland followed along the course of the River Alun through Llandegla, Llanarmon to Mold. The area from Valle Crucis to Llanarmon has changed so little since 1536 that it is possible to follow Leland's footsteps and to understand his enthusiasm. There were no maps and his Itinerary was one of true exploration.

This is the route of the horse – track taken by Leland
on his way from Valle Crucis to the summit (at 1367 feet above sea level)
of the Bwlch yr Oernant (pass) which pre-dated the Horseshoe Pass.
It is steeper than 1 in 3 and leads from the Dee basin into that of the River Alun.

POSTSCRIPT

During the summers of 1535-45 Leland spent his time travelling the length and breadth of England and Wales visiting parts of each county. The rest of the year he spent in London and at the rectory at Thame, Oxfordshire. There is no information about his family life or whether he was married but two brothers are known. By the end of 1545 he started to write up his notes on his travels and presented them to Henry VIII on 1st January 1546. Because of serious illness this was to be the last full year of the King's life. He died in 1547 and Leland was reported as having a serious mental illness. His close friend, John Bale, described him as being 'mad' and would today have been diagnosed as a manic-depressive. He was placed in the custody of his elder brother in London. John Bale gathered his notes together and produced in 1549 the 'Laborious Journey and Serche for England's Antiquities' by John Leland. The causes of Leland's illness are unknown – perhaps spite from his enemies, overwork, an overwrought passion or obsession with collecting or even vainglory. It may have been the result of his sense of failure at not producing a literary success as a poet. He died on 8th April 1552 and was buried in London but his gravestone or 'monument' was lost in the 'Great Fire' of London 1555.

However it is fortunate that the manuscripts of his journeys were copied by the antiquary, John Stow (in 1576), before they had been damaged – each folio or page was numbered only on the front and some were stained by damp and in places the ink had faded. A few years later, in 1612, the manuscript found its way to William Burton, an historian, who in 1634 gave seven of the eight volumes of the 'Itinerary' to the Bodleian Library, Oxford. In 1710-12 Thomas Hearne, Record Keeper of the Bodleian, printed and published the manuscripts. In 1906-10 Lucy Toulmin Smith completed a fine edition in five volumes of the 'Itinerary' and also brought together the journeys in Wales (1536-39) with all the place-names in the original spelling. She added footnotes in an attempt to identify their modern names but there are serious problems with the Welsh names which Leland was unable to understand because of their pronunciation. Near Wrexham he writes *'John Puleston, serjeant at arms, has a manor-house, within half a mile of Wrexham, at Marsche.'*

'Marsche' was Leland's version of 'Plas ym Mers' which is now 'Lower Berse'. Similarly, in another Puleston house, at Overton, Leland referred

Ewloe Castle – showing the keep or Welsh Tower and in foreground the castle well. Completed in 1257 by Llywelyn ap Gruffudd. Was a ruin in Leland's day at a place called 'Castel Yollo'.

A Garderobe (lavatory) projecting from an external wall – Beaumaris Castle. Medieval sense of humour!

to *'Edward Puleston, son of the Knight, lives in Overton parish at Coitegolle'* which, again, is a misunderstanding of the Welsh pronunciation of 'Coedgoleu'. Later this word itself was lost, in the Anglicised border region, and was replaced by 'Lightwood' which is a literal translation of 'Coedgoleu'.

Practically all of the names mentioned by Leland still exist and when they are plotted on a map of northern Wales they give a fairly coherent plan of his route. It is probable that he entered northern Wales from Oswestry and from the border region of Maelor Saesneg travelled on horseback to the extremity of the Llŷn peninsula. He may have ended the journey at Penrhyndeudraeth. Although he describes the coast southwards through Harlech to Machynlleth he gives little eye-witness evidence that he took this route. He may have retraced his steps and after reaching Rhuddlan entered Flintshire at Bodfari where he mentions Mr Powell who was 'a gentleman of Flintshire, who by ancient custom, gave the badge of a silver harp to the best harpist in northern Wales'.

Powell, who lived at Penrhyn Old Hall which Leland had visited on his west-bound journey also had *'a ruinous castle, or pile, at a place called Castel Yollo (Ewloe Castle) which is two miles from Northop village, a little on the left-hand side of the highway to Chester'.*

The route from Bodfari to Northop followed the easy route ('highway') to Chester and he would have noticed the fine church at Northop, one of the 'Stanley' churches which he had seen and recorded at Holt, Gresford and Mold, built in the previous reign of Henry VII. These stunning churches were all built of local sandstone ('the parish rock'). The absence of a reference to Northop Church is an interesting omission perhaps explained by his 'tour' of northern Wales ending and his county-by-county itinerary of England about to begin – 1539.

AN ARCHAELOGICAL AFTERTHOUGHT

Apart from Denbigh castle the oldest surviving building in Denbigh is the black and white timber house – now Siop Clwyd – at 33 High Street. It is a narrow, two-storeyed building on the north side of High Street which was then the market square. It was constructed in 1533 with evidence provided by a study of tree-rings (dendrochronology) in three joists which support the ground floor ceiling. A core was drilled through each beam to give an exact sequence of the annual tree-rings from the heartwood to the bark. The cores were sanded with progressively fine sand-paper to reveal the ring sequence. One beam had sixty-one rings and from the 'bar-code' matching the rings to known dates the life history of the tree from its 'birth' to the date it was felled could be exactly estimated. The beam was taken from an oak tree which started its life in AD 1473 and from its sixty-one rings and barkwood it was felled in AD 1533. It was then used to build the house at No 33 shortly afterwards and was therefore only three or four years before Leland's visit to Denbigh. If he visited the market which was held every Tuesday he would have seen the new house, It is probably shown on John Speed's map (1610) as one of a block of four houses facing the High Cross at the centre of the market square. Denbigh was rapidly expanding outside the medieval walls below the castle in Leland's time and No 33 was part of this building programme.

Siop Clwyd, 33 High Street, Denbigh
Built in the time of Leland.

Part of the High Cross which stood in the
centre of the Market Square Denbigh.

APPENDIX

Leland's Itinerary

MOLESDALE YN WALSCH CAULLID STREDALEN

In Molesdale is but one greate paroche caullid Plouhe (paroche) Wriothegrig, of sum communely Molesdale, there longe 3. chappelles onto it. Sum say that Molesdale was ons a market toune. There be 2. fayres yet kept at Molesdale, but the wekely market is decayed. Yet it hath the name of a maire, and a great numbre of houses be withowt token almost destroyed, and there hath beene 2. streates, as Streate Byle, and Streate Dadlede in Walsch, in Englisch the Court House Streate, byside other litle lanes. Now in al be scant 40. houses. At the north ende of Byle Streate appere diches and hilles yn tokyn of an auncient castel or building there. It is now caullid Mont Brenebyley, and on the side of it is a fayre springe. Alen Ryver cummith withyn a bou shot of Molesdale Chirche. And at the southe ende of the towne is a rylle caullid Houne, and sone after rennith into Alen.

Robert Edwardes a gentylman dwellith at . . . on the Flintshire side of Alen yn Molesdale, having plenty of wood and goodly medow by Alen side. The wood thens is caried to Chestre a vi. miles of.

Moste parte of the paroch is meately level ground, having beside other thinges very good corne. And there be cole pittes a 3. quarters of a mile from Molesdale toune.

Ithel (*Angl.* Ellys) Griffith dwellith on the north side, scant a quarter of a mile from Molesdale toune at a place caullid Lloen (grove) Egrine.

John Wenne ap Roberte dwellid at a stone tower caullid Broncoit, alias Regnaultes Towre, 3. quarters of a mile from Molesdale toune. There cummith a litle ryllet by this square toure caullid . . . and a quarter of a myle beneth the tour goith into Alen descending from west to este.

There is a nother water in Molesdale caullid Avon Terrig almost as byg as Alen. Yet goyng from west to north est it goith ynto Alen. Terrig Ryver cummith thorough a peace of Yale or it cum into Molesdale.

There be other smaulle ryllettys yn Molesdale. So that by springges and rylles this paroch beyng yn lenght a v. myles is wel sevid of water and of dyvers other good thinges.

Molesdale lyith north on Hopesdale, and Yale lyeth west on it. Flyntshire lyith north on it, and Ardin by est.

The Tower, Broncoed, Mold.

ACKNOWLEDGEMENTS

I am indebted to the generosity of people who have allowed me to visit their homes and photograph their houses. I visited houses from the Borders – Captain and Mrs Myddelton of New Hall, Chirk – to the remotest part of the Llŷn Peninsula at Rhosgyll Fawr where Mr & Mrs Colin Randall live.

Four of my maps were professionally drawn by Ken Lloyd Gruffydd of Mold.

I am also indebted to the following official bodies –

Bodleian Library, University of Oxford and the shelfmark;
MS. Top Gen. e. 12, fol. 37v
Royal Commission of Ancient & Historical Monuments (Aberystwyth)
Clwyd-Powys Archaeological Trust (Welshpool)
Record Offices at Dolgellau, Caernarfon, Llangefni, Ruthin, A.N. Palmer Centre at Wrexham, Flintshire County Library (Mold)
The vicars of Clynnog-fawr, Llanengan, Ruabon, Holt and Ysbyty Ifan were kind enough to give me access to their churches.
Gillian Fraser (for the library copy of Leland's manuscript.)
Charles Wynne Eyton (who allowed me to photograph his house - The Tower in Mold)
Phill Ebbrill

I am especially grateful to Min Drinkwater of Top Type (Mold) for typing the manuscript and to Myrddin ap Dafydd for advice and guidance.

FURTHER READING:

John Leland's Itinerary: Travels in Tudor England
John Chandler, Gloucestershire, 1998
The Itinerary of John Leland in or about the years 1535-1543
Lucy Toulmin-Smith (Ed), foreword by
Thomas Kendrick, London, 1964
Preliminary tree-ring analysis of timbers from selected buildings in Denbigh, report by Nigel Nayling.